The Evolution
of
EMILY

The Campbell Homestead

by Emily Lewis Miles
with Jervis F. Russell

First Edition 1981
© Copyright 1981

Creative Communications

Published by:

Printed by:
Olympic Graphic Arts, Inc.
Forks, Washington 98331

LIBRARY OF CONGRESS
CATALOG CARD NO.
81-71055
Miles
Evolution of Emily

Washington: Creative Communications

ISBN 0-939116-06-5

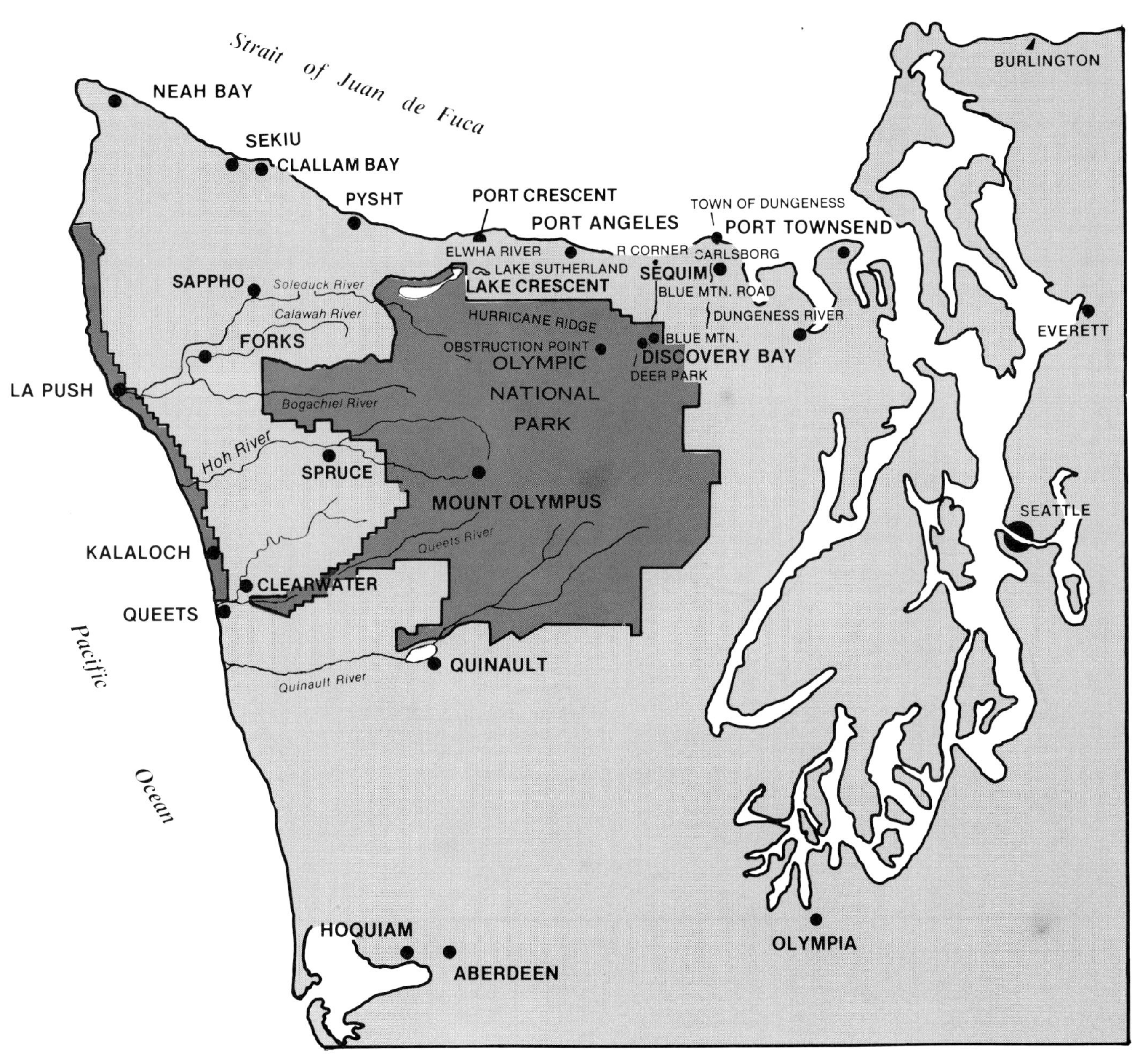

Strait of Juan de Fuca
NEAH BAY
SEKIU
CLALLAM BAY
PYSHT
BURLINGTON
PORT CRESCENT
PORT ANGELES
TOWN OF DUNGENESS
PORT TOWNSEND
ELWHA RIVER
R CORNER
CARLSBORG
SAPPHO
Soleduck River
LAKE SUTHERLAND
LAKE CRESCENT
SEQUIM
BLUE MTN. ROAD
Calawah River
HURRICANE RIDGE
DUNGENESS RIVER
EVERETT
FORKS
OBSTRUCTION POINT
OLYMPIC
BLUE MTN.
DISCOVERY BAY
LA PUSH
Bogachiel River
NATIONAL
DEER PARK
Hoh River
PARK
SPRUCE
MOUNT OLYMPUS
KALALOCH
Queets River
SEATTLE
CLEARWATER
QUEETS
Pacific
QUINAULT
Quinault River
Ocean
HOQUIAM
ABERDEEN
OLYMPIA

DEDICATION

TO MY LITTLE MOTHER

JENNIE E. CAMPBELL

COVER:

The azaleas on the cover were reproduced from a painting done by Emily's father and given to her when she was a child. They represent her middle name, Azalea. Emily has cherished the painting for more than seventy-five years.

ACKNOWLEDGEMENTS

Thanks to Bert Kellogg, Clallam County Museum and Olympic National Park for many of the photographs contributed. Our gratitude also to John Somers and Lloyd Beebe for photos, other photos were provided by the author and her husband, Roscoe Miles. The cooperation of typographer Scott Price is appreciated.

A companion book to
THE IRON MAN OF THE HOH,
THE MAN NOT THE MYTH.

PREFACE

This is Emily's story. But more than that it is the growing up of a girl and a woman, and a frontier. The pioneers to the Far-west frontier caused it to grow by learning to deal with, and overcome, a climate and geography unknown in their eastern homelands. Emily, the girl, survived being born into the age of Victorian naiveness, became a wiser young woman of the post World War I 1920s and a freer mature woman of post World War II days.

The woman of her early life was expected to see, first, only through her parents' eyes, then only through the vision of her husband. Their worlds were hers.

Emily Lewis Miles did what was expected. But with a spirit, humor and love that prepared her for feminine freedom when it finally arrived in the far northwest corner of the nation.

Through it all, that spirit, humor and love remained intact. The result is a fulfillment of freedom without the loss of the inherent qualities of femininity.

The Evolution of Emily is a true story. It was first told in a brief manuscript by the subject herself. In months of discussion and memory searching it was filled out with my help, but in Emily's words.

It is a revelation of frontier life, of a battle waged by a mother and four children in a man's world, of ability of neighbors to live together in harmony.

But most of all it is the story of a successful woman—Emily.

—Jervis F. Russell

CONTENTS

The Campbell youngsters—Earline, Francis, Alfred and Emily (at piano)

Chapter 1   An Introduction

In 1902 Sears, Roebuck and Company of Chicago, Illinois, ("Cheapest Supply House on Earth") offered its "highest of high grade" bicycles for $15.75—a Napoleon model for the men and the Josephine for the ladies.

Sears sold a cabinet-type sewing machine for $10.45, a wood-burning heater was offered for $3.80. A "long bosom shirt" for men was 40 cents, the most expensive ladies' shoe (a cloth top patent vici) was priced at $2.95, the best men's shoe was priced the same, and men could buy a three-piece suit for $7.50 but if they wanted to go first class with "Bushendorff's Imported German Cloth" the cost went up to $20.

The granddaddy of mail order houses had seen the infinite market of the growing West and it was beating off all competitors to provide rural America with a department store no farther away than the local post office.

Little Emily Campbell of Harvey, Illinois, just outside Chicago, could have figuratively stood with her back to the giant mail order house and watched the 1902 catalogues fan out over the nation. But three months before the year arrived Emily would be at the receiving edge of that fan—in the extreme northwest corner of the United States.

President William McKinley was shot down in 1901 and Vice President Theodore Roosevelt became President. Roosevelt in the White House meant the Panama Canal would be built. The Progressive Era of the United States had begun.

None of those things meant anything to Emily in 1901, or possibly at any other time. She was only seven years old. But it wasn't just age that limited the area of her world.

All of us have our life-boundaries. Teddy Roosevelt was only confined by the world. He was born to it and reveled in it all his life. He hunted in Africa, fought in Cuba, and sent the United States Navy around the world. Why not? He had money, an established family to launch him, and an expansionist mind.

Not so Emily. Emily Campbell's world was shrunken by the confining boundaries of economics and a conservative society. The immediate effort needed to maintain family finances allowed little time to look at far horizons. Her mother was born of foreign parents, was a divorcee, and she worked for a living—all grounds for suspicion in the days of unbridled bigotry and unliberated femininity.

Oh, in 1901 she was married, all right. But to an unproven artist, a fact that could increase instead of decrease suspicion.

Nevertheless, Emily was to have her bit of "expansionism." Sears, Roebuck and Company was not the only one to feel the beckoning of the West. For a good part of the preceding century sweating oxen and horses, smoking locomotives and billowing sails had been straining to move the dreamers and adventurous westward.

Some were drawn to the golden fantasy of California, others to the farmlands and cattle ranges of the prairies. By 1901 much of that land was taken. But that provided no problem for the determined. (Being a little gullible helped too.) There was still land left in the extreme Northwest, where most people didn't even know land existed. True, many of them had heard of Seattle and Puget Sound but the West didn't stop there. Still farther westward was the Olympic Peninsula.

That lopsided rectangle of land with a center of snowy mountain peaks was far less likely to be known—unless the promoters for the railroads or the remote, new frontier communities had gotten within earshot. The images created by these hucksters were glorified enough to make a preacher rob the poor box and head west on a unicycle.

One booklet published and distributed by a group formed to entice the easterners to pack their baggage described dairying possibilities in the Promised Land. "This country is one of the very best for making butter and cheese because in summer the weather is cool, an abundance of pure running water is found on nearly every farm, and the cows feed in rich, green pastures from early spring until late in the fall . . . ."

What the promoter *didn't* write was that the "abundance of pure running water" could get so abundant it would often wash cows and farm right down to the Strait of Juan de Fuca and into the ocean. And it failed to note the rain that was the source of the "abundance" came in summer as well as winter and could ruin a crop of hay, if it didn't stop it from growing in the first place. On one edge of the deluge area was a near-desert prairie. Emily would spend most of her life where one climate ended and the other started—with some of the benefits, and many of the curses, of both.

The booklet said "good butter will always sell here at a good price." It didn't say how many of the people were too poor to buy it and that the bigger markets were a two-day roundtrip by steamer away.

As for educational facilities, the book very honestly attested to the fact that "there is not a community of any considerable size in the whole territory that is without its free school from three to 10 month a year." What it didn't tell the comfortable Midwest family sitting around its kitchen table and warmed by the heat radiating from the massive, ornate cookstove (to save heating the parlor) was that "a community of any considerable size" was a rarity on the Olympic Peninsula.

It was at the very least exaggeration to write, "It is not uncommon to see apple blossoms and strawberry blossoms as late as December, and large ripe strawberries." The writer must have had eyesight reaching all the way to sunny California. By December any strawberries would likely be dissolved in the Olympic Peninsula's consistent winter rains.

A sharp-eyed reader would have tallied a rainfall chart contained in the booklet to find almost 50 inches fell in the year recorded—and you can bet that was considered a favorable year by the promoters. Annual rainfall on the Peninsula ranges from fifteen inches (too dry) in the most arid area to ten times that much (too wet) in the dampest region.

But what distracted the eyes of the dreamers from reality was undoubtably a paragraph headed "Homestead." It said, "Every person being 21 years of age, or the head of a family, and a citizen of the United States, or who has declared his intention to become such, can enter 100 (sic) acres of unappropriated government land. And by residing upon it continuously . . . and improving it for five years, if he is then a full citizen, upon due proof of such residence, cultivation and citizenship, the government will issue him a patent for the land which makes it absolutely his own. The land fees &c. (costs) usually amount to about $30." Free land!

One hundred and sixty acres of other "unappropriated government land" could be purchased for $1.25 per acre by just "erecting a dwelling thereon and inhabiting and improving the same in good faith for six months," the publication promised.

What that Midwestern family sitting around that table by lamplight *did* know was the Big Bosses of industry in cities were treating them like puppets on a string, keeping their income marginal, certainly throttling their opportunity for control over their own destiny.

The answer to all this (or so it seemed) was contained in the misleading words of such booklets and the mesmerizing oration of the hucksters. The infinite image of a man standing alongside his wife and children, surveying the fulfillment of the works of their own hands, their own master of all they surveyed, so to speak; that was the dream drawn for the dreamers.

George Campbell, Emily's father, knew all about drawing. He was an artist. Maybe that made him more susceptible to the dream verbally illustrated by the hucksters, maybe he just had wandering feet; maybe he could envision the beauty of the Far West as he visualized his art work before he put a stroke of paint on canvas.

If he perceived the beauty on the Olympic Peninsula his vision was accurate. Greenish-blue saltwater almost completely encloses its six thousand square miles—larger than Connecticut, smaller than New Jersey. Forming the west side is the rolling, roily Pacific Ocean. Capping the north, forming a swayback border with Canada's Vancouver Island, is the Strait of Juan de Fuca. Hood Canal, a spur of the Strait, cuts south, leaving only a neck of land at the south to keep the Peninsula from being an island.

Timbered hillsides rise from sea level to elevations of five thousand to six thousand feet where they become stark, snowcovered peaks topped by Mount Olympus that stretches for a height of eight thousand feet.

The land sought by the homesteader was in the valleys along the rivers tumbling from the peaks, or along the rim of fertile ground bordering the seas' shores.

It was the inundating green of the country that should have caused the arriving land-seeker to catch the next boat back east. (It would have to be a boat to Seattle; there were no roads or tracks connecting the Peninsula to the rest of the nation.)

The green was mothered by unpredictable waves of precipitation rolling ashore from storm centers over the ocean. They seldom stopped for long, sometimes dampening the usually drier months of July and August and almost disappearing for weeks in mid-winter. The saying was, "Only a fool or a stranger predicts the weather on the Olympic Peninsula."

The constantly changing, unforecastable weather made farming a game of Russian Roulette. The farmer pulled the trigger when he planted; he hoped the hammer hit a chamber of moderate weather. If it didn't and there was no money for a second planting, or if it too failed, disaster struck.

What made farm crops uncertain made nature's crops thrive. Stout timber towered to two-hundred and fifty feet and beneath it the more tender vegetation formed a lush floor.

By the time the Campbells arrived logging was established as an industry that would tide over many homesteaders and provide fulltime occupation for others.

The niche of the Peninsula selected by, or more accurately for, the Campbells was in a hillside along the Strait of Juan de Fuca. Eighty miles to the southeast the Puget Sound port of Seattle had become a jumping off place for the wealth of Alaska and was destined to be the commerce center of the Northwest. Eighty miles to the west the village of the Makah Indians marked the last bit of land before the Pacific Ocean.

The objective of the Campbells was Port Angeles. It could be said it had been selected for instead of by them because of the influence of Norman Smith. It was his father who is credited with establishing Port Angeles. In the days before logging and commercial fishing the existence of the town depended on wrestling the U.S. Custom House from Port Townsend forty miles east, something Norman's father, Victor, did by steaming into its harbor with an armed ship and demanding the Custom House papers be turned over.

Although the Port Angeles site of the Custom House was eventually destroyed by a flooding stream and the town's father was later lost at sea, Port Angeles got a new boost when the socialistic-patterned Puget Sound Cooperative Colony arrived to build a mill, hotel and other buildings in the 1880s. Norman, who was the town's second mayor, carried on his father's efforts for the growth of Port Angeles, but with the power of speech instead of an armed ship.

When Mrs. Campbell and the four children arrived in 1901 (Mr. Campbell would arrive later) the town's businesses were housed in rustic wooden buildings crowded along the waterfront, many on pilings to allow the tide to move in and out at will. The forested hills that rose directly to the mountains began with a bluff almost at water's edge, forcing the overlapping of the structures and the sea.

A wharf extended into the water the farthest and welcomed the small steamers arriving from Seattle and ports en route. From the extreme western end of the town a giant finger of sand and rock curled out from the mainland to provide a barrier on the north against the storm-driven waves from the Strait that would otherwise slash at the town's frail business community. Near the end of what was named Ediz Hook a lighthouse warned off ships.

Along portions of the beach not yet covered with buildings, peaceful Indians brought ashore their canoes dug out of cedar logs. They pitched their tents and sold salmon fresh-caught in the Strait and baskets woven from native grasses and artistically decorated with dyes known only to the Indians.

The residences were scattered up the hillside south. Port Angeles was designated the nation's second national city (Washington, D.C. was the first) by Abraham Lincoln during the Civil War. Later the federal land was opened to homesteading and the national claim relinquished.

The town divided the Peninsula's wettest land from its driest. Westward, the annual precipitation increased. A "rain shadow" caused by the mountains ringing the water from inland bound clouds resulted in increasingly drier conditions to the east. Yearly rainfall in the area sixty miles west, where the community of Forks was located, reached one hundred and fifty inches. Sequim, fifteen miles east of Port Angeles averaged seventeen inches, so dry that farming was not practical without irrigation.

It was between Sequim and Port Angeles that Emily would spend most of her life. And it is from there she tells her story:

All five children before leaving Illinois; Alfred and Francis Stevenson and Emily, Earline and Hubert Campbell

Chapter 2

It was your kids and my kids, and they were all our kids.

I was born February 15, 1894, in Harvey, Illinois, to George and Jennie Campbell. My sister Earline was born April 5, 1895. We had three half-brothers: Mama had two boys by a former marriage, Alfred and Francis Stevenson, and there was Dad's boy Hubert by his former marriage.

Mama had been divorced and Dad's wife had died when they both ended up doing photo retouching for Chicago Portrait Company. It was the first time they had met but before long their capacity for romance brought on a second blooming and they were married.

It was just before the turn of the century and during a depression, and the big talk was about going west where the land was fresh and fertile and so were opportunities.

In 1900, Norman Smith came to Harvey. He was the son of the ''Father of Port Angeles.'' He was also the town's greatest early promoter—a one man Chamber of Commerce for the settlement in northwestern Washington State.

During one of his tours Smith stopped off at Harvey, just to be sure everyone knew about his Promised Land. Dad was there and within a few months we were ex-residents of Illinois.

It was September 1901 when Mama, my sister Earline and I and our two half-brothers, Alfred, fourteen, and Francis, twelve, left Harvey by train for Port Angeles. Dad stayed to sell the house and ship our furniture and Hubert remained with his aunt where he would make his home until he was fifteen.

Mama was thrifty and Earline and I were small for our age. The combination got the two of us to the West free. Mama would watch for the conductor to come up the aisle between the seats of the coach. When she spotted him she would let us know and we would shrink even smaller by pulling our feet under us, hunching down in the seat, and slipping on baby bonnets. Children under six didn't pay. Earline was six and I was seven.

Finances didn't allow for eating in dining cars either. We brought our meals with us already prepared, as many others did. The food, combined with crowded conditions and a lack of washing and bathing facilities, resulted in some very ripe aromas.

It wasn't long before we began to smell something specially bad. Mama was sure it was the family in front of us that caused the smell. Anyway, it didn't take the passengers long to get past our division of seats. It seemed to get worse as we rumbled over the hot prairies.

My brother Francis, who was always hungry and who was always ahead of time and had already joined the modern ways of ''help yourself,'' was the one to discover the source of the smell. The discovery came when he went to sneak a snack out of one of our food baskets. The chickens mother had fried back in Harvey, and we had been eating early in the trip but left untouched for a while, had lost their battle to stay edible, or even bearable.

The train took us to Seattle. From there on the route was on water—from Puget Sound out into the Strait of Juan de Fuca which connects the Pacific Ocean and the Sound.

We came to Port Angeles on a passenger boat named the *Alice Gertrude*, a small steamer of the Mosquito Fleet that provided a way to get to where roads didn't yet go.

When Mama, who had spent most of her life in the big city of Chicago, saw the moss-covered roofs of the few houses that passed for Port Angeles she was ready to tie us four kids together, jump in the bay, and try to swim back to Seattle. But even if she had accomplished that she was too nearly broke to buy tickets for Illinois.

It was pouring rain. We were wet. Mama was crying. We girls were hanging onto each other. It wasn't just the tide that was at a low ebb. Then a man named Ed Christoferson came up to us where we stood and persuaded Mama to take rooms in the hotel he owned. It was called the Globe Hotel and was the best in town.

But even the best didn't have heat in the rooms, only a pot-bellied stove downstairs. It didn't take Mama long to get out the long-handled underwear for us kids even though we didn't wear them in Illinois till the temper-

Mosquito fleet

ature hit zero. The rain that never seemed to stop in the winter and the cold wind off the Strait added to the cold.

The rain eventually stopped and like all kids we were ready to go exploring the minute the drops quit spotting the puddles.

The Christofersons had one child, a boy named Roy. Roy was like a lot of our modern children whose mothers work outside the home—he could get away with murder. He was quite a prize to us. He knew some interesting places and offered to show us around.

The tide was out and that was a treat. On the beach in front of town Roy showed us how to dig clams and find pretty rocks. Business buildings on the waterfront hung out over the tideland, supported on pilings.

Roy took us girls under the Guttenberg Furniture Store. It was all open under there. He told us we might find things that dropped from the store up above. What he didn't tell us was that the sanitary disposal system of waterfront stores was the tide. It did the flushing as it came in and out. The toilets emptied right onto the beach.

Well, we found things that dropped from the building all right—and some of them squished over the tops of shoes. That was the first and last trip with Roy. He had

Port Angeles built over tidewater

Port Angeles, 1897

initiated us to Port Angeles.

Every day Mama went out looking for a house to rent. In Illinois we had a nine-room home. In Port Angeles there were few real houses to rent. There were many empty shacks, as Mama called them. They were left by the short-timers who had found conditions not to their liking and had moved on.

It took a week of looking but Mama managed to find a big house on Pine Hill, a high point in the west end of town. Port Angeles was built on several such ridges separated from each other by creeks which cut deep valleys as the streams flowed from the high rising mountains bordering Port Angeles on the south and on down through town to empty into the Strait on the north.

Our new home, the Hatfield Place, had a kitchen, dining room, living room and a bedroom downstairs, and four bedrooms upstairs. In back was a woodshed with an attached privy, something considered by us to be quite different than the solitary outhouses standing behind other homes.

After our stay in the hotel, it was a hungry and sleepy Mama and kids that moved the few belongings we had into the house. Dad had not yet sent the furniture from Harvey. The first thing Mama ordered was wood for the stove. We had been so cold at the hotel.

It was time for school and Earline and I didn't have far to go, just a few blocks to the Pine Hill Schoolhouse where a playfield donated by the Elks Lodge is now located.

Francis and Alfred weren't so fortunate. For Francis it wasn't too bad. He had to walk west down into Tumwater Valley then up Tumwater Hill, now called Lincoln Heights, to a one-room building standing where Lincoln School was later built, about a mile. Alfred went the other direction to old Central School, clear across town, where Washington Elementary School was later constructed and where the post office is currently

Pine Hill School

Ship in Port Angeles Harbor

located. That was nearly a two-mile walk.

But walking was a way of life then. Work and play were both a matter of walking. Those were happy and adventurous days to us greenhorns from the Midwest, and walking provided that adventure every Saturday, when it didn't rain.

Our favorite Saturday hikes were either down the hill to the beach along the Strait of Juan de Fuca or up Tumwater Creek to where the town got its water. Most of the time it was just Mama and us girls that took the hikes. The boys must have had work to do.

Port Angeles has a harbor partially enclosed by a neck of sand and gravel that curves out from the beach on the west end of town and provides an arm to protect the harbor from the sometimes boisterous winds and waves driving in from the Pacific.

Crews of Navy ships, lumber schooners, and the small passenger steamers were among seafarers seeking shelter behind Ediz Hook, or ''the Spit'' as it was more commonly called.

Dressed in our other-than-Sunday clothes—long stockings, gingham dresses, coats, and high-buttoned shoes—we started out.

The trail from Pine Hill began in a gentle slope down through stands of willow and alder trees till it reached the brink of the hill above the creek. The way got steep at that point and the path became a zig-zag down the near-cliff to Tumwater Creek then meandered along the stream to its mouth. Once on the flat area along the beach the adventure began.

The first thing after turning west toward the Spit was a small farm with a few fruit trees and several cows. It was like an outpost. Beyond it was the sand and sea that contained mystery and wonder to us ''foreigners'' from inland.

A dark, still lagoon lay at the point where the Spit joined the mainland. We hurried along its shore with a feeling of dread of the known and unknown. We had seen devil fish, with their tenacles beckoning us as they flowed over the rocks beneath the surface. Lord only knows what else made its home in the depths. If it matched our imaginations we were happier not knowing.

Once past the lagoon the world became brighter. The cold saltwater crashed in waves against the sand, and beyond those waves were miles of open water ending with the outline of Canada's hills across from us and the ocean to the west.

On the beach were knickknacks that made searching the sands more exciting for a child than browsing the counters of a dime-store. There were shells of all shapes and pebbles of all hues. There were little crabs and bits of wood polished as the waves constantly shuffled them

Mama and girls race on Ediz Hook beach, 1901.

against the sand.

It wasn't just us girls who were attracted to products of the beach. Mama enjoyed collecting rocks and shells as much as we did. She took them home and sent them east to friends who had trouble comprehending the wonders of the Northwest. She also used her artistic ability to paint scenes of the region and send to the Midwesterners.

The Strait of Juan de Fuca had properties other than entertainment. Mama viewed the waters, that were bitter cold even in summer, as being able to do what medical men have not been able to do to this day—cure the common cold.

When we contacted a sniffle the cure was simple. Mama simply made us submerge in the icy seawater, letting the waves smack us on the back. We were then wiped off with a towel and rushed home as fast as we could go.

Mama depended a lot on unusual ways of treating ailments. She relied on Christian Science and faith healers at times. It seemed she was always involved with some kind of illness, although I don't remember much mention of what they were diagnosed to be. She couldn't wash clothes, couldn't churn butter, but when she got upset at something we did, Mama found the strength to whip us—and hard.

Not any more than five-foot, two inches tall and weighing no more than 102 pounds, Mama maintained discipline. She stood straight and stern, always dressed as a lady, with a combed switch (an arrangement of false hair) hiding the fact her hair was sparse. Much of her manner could have been because of her background, Mama's father had been a German count.

The outings had yet another purpose. If we had not taken a cure that day and could walk home more leisurely, we would stop along the way and pick horsetail ferns (or rushes), a forerunner of steelwool for scouring pots and pans.

The scene was completely changed if Mama decided we should go up Tumwater Creek to the "waterworks."

That route was through a tunnel of tall timber—giant cedar, hemlock and fir. At the end of the trail was a dam and a spillway filling the main waterline supplying Port Angeles.

In season there were berries to eat and the crowded, green, rain-fed ground-cover of ferns, salal, mosses, flowers and other plants beneath the trees to fill the senses with the wonder of it all.

As happened on the explorations to the beach, there was a picnic lunch before returning home. Mama picknicked all over the country.

The hikes got fewer as winter came closer but a new pleasure began to fill our thoughts. Dad was to arrive by

Christmas.

Mama was most excited, but we kids came close to matching her anticipation. Then came the bad news—Dad wouldn't make it by Christmas. Selling the house and packing the furniture had taken longer than expected.

Well, if Dad couldn't get home for Christmas, Christmas would have to wait for Dad.

Christmas and Dad arrived at the Campbell house in January. When the great day came, the family dressed in its finest and walked over ridges and through the valleys to the downtown waterfront.

When Dad stepped off the boat, he received an outburst of welcoming kisses and hugs stored under pressure for six husbandless, fatherless months. Then home to a long-delayed Christmas tree strung with chains of colored paper.

Dad George Campbell

Mama Jennie at 57

Chapter 3

Right after Dad and us kids in Mama's affections came her piano. It arrived with Dad and life became more normal, as well as complete. However, there were some problems, as could be expected in a family of six.

In early spring, smallpox broke out in the schools and students had to be vaccinated or stay home, so Mama kept us home. She didn't believe in vaccinating.

There were many one-room vacant shacks on Pine Hill, providing us girls with lots of playhouses while we were out of school. One of them was much nicer than the others. It had a stove, a little table and a shelf of medicines. The medicines gave my sister Earline an idea.

She had watched how vaccinations were given—just scratch the skin and put a drop of medicine on the scratch. So she scratched my arm, put some stuff out of one of the medicine bottles on it, and in a few days any doctor would have taken it for the real thing. It really "took," as they say.

That was the way it was with Earline and me all of our lives—still is. She would come up with some prank or other devilment and I believed everything she said. No matter how outlandish the story she told, I swallowed it whole. She stayed ahead of Mama too. Earline was strong willed. She wasn't about to let Mama get the best of her.

I missed a lot of breakfasts because of my sister. We had to take a sponge-bath every morning, and if we weren't finished before time for breakfast we went without eating. The more Mama would scold at Earline, the less likely she was to finish her sponge-bath in time. And I was foolish enough to go right along with her.

Earline was nervy. She had backbone and was always ready for fun. And she was popular with boys. Everything seemed to come easy for her. She wasn't studious but had no trouble with school studies.

Dad had found work cutting timber for the Forrester-Tuttle Shingle Mill on Klondike Hill, now called Black Diamond, on the southern outskirts of town, but he broke his watch while falling a tree so he quit. Anyway, it was time to carry out the plan Norman Smith had planted in Dad's mind back in Harvey, Illinois—starting a new life on new land.

Shortly after arriving in Port Angeles Mama had let it be known she was looking for property to build on. Christoferson, the hotel owner, had suggested a real estate agent. The agent picked us up in a buggy and took us sixteen miles east of town to the Blue Mountain area. He showed Mama a homestead that its owner was willing to sell rights to.

It wasn't much but Mama agreed to buy it.

A one-room log cabin about fifteen feet by twenty feet squatted in a small clearing. There was only one door and no windows. Nearby was a half-acre field. The field and the area around the cabin were the only cleared land on the 160 acres. The rest was tall timber and brush. The only crop was one common to homesteads whose owners looked for a simple produce to fit the requirements of proving-up on their federally-granted land. The garden contained nothing but Jerusalem artichokes, which reseed themselves each year.

Now, with Dad not working, construction of a new house on the property started. In some ways it reflected the fact Dad was an artist and that he and his sons were hard workers, but none of them were carpenters.

The house the Campbell family built

Eight-foot cedar logs were split in half and stood upright side by side to make the walls of one story. Another row made the walls of the top story. It was an uncommon practice, and Dad never did figure how to satisfactorily close in the corners. But soon it was a forty-foot square home with half of the interior finished.

With a plan in mind of having a place for Dad to paint, a studio was built onto the top floor.

The forty by twenty portion that was more or less complete had a kitchen at one end and a front room with a wood-burning heater at the other. For quite a while we slept in the front room, then Francis and Alfred put in a ceiling and three bedrooms upstairs.

Artists were in short demand out West so Dad had trouble finding work. He heard the federal government needed a coat of paint on the lighthouse and buildings at Tatoosh Island where the Strait of Juan de Fuca meets the Pacific. Dad got the contract and worked there six weeks. During a period of bad weather when he couldn't work on the buildings Dad rowed to the mainland and painted a picture of a rock arch formation. The picture was beautiful.

Dad did get paid for two paintings. Dr. Donald McGillivray, who helped found a hospital in Port Angeles, asked Dad to do the paintings. I remember one was of the doctor's St. Bernard dog. With the money Dad went to Seattle to find work that fit his skills.

We would only see him one more time.

During the several months Dad was gone Mama suffered from a growth on her arm. She asked a faith healer to treat it. It was necessary for them to be alone during some of the treatment. That was all it took for an evil-minded former friend to start malicious gossip that was relayed to Dad as soon as he got home.

Looking back we kids could see something was wrong when Mama and Dad took a long walk the morning after he got home, but we never knew for sure what happened between them. I heard Dad apologize to Mama several times at breakfast for doubting her, then he left. Only occasionally did we hear about him after that. I was only nine years old at the time, and I really loved him.

Emily: Nine years old

By this time Earline was eight years old, Alfred was sixteen, Francis was fourteen. Things were pretty tough for a while. Even getting an education was a problem.

To prove up on a homestead it was only required that a homesteader stay on the land six months of the year so we lived in town parts of the winters, but not long enough to get the schooling we needed. School was in session all winter in town but only summers at Blue Mountain. Earline and I found it hard to get out of first grade. We seemed to never get enough schooling at one time to move into second.

During one of the stays at the homestead, Alfred found work at the Forrester-Tuttle Mill. It was a twenty-mile walk. He would get home Saturday night around midnight, after a six-day week. We would all still be up waiting for him.

The roof of the house was only partly finished, so Francis learned how to split shakes out of blocks of cedar and the two boys would put shakes on the roof on Sundays.

Francis later got a job at the Forrester-Tuttle Mill and in 1904 both boys worked there.

Alfred's first job at the mill had been helping in the kitchen. The men called him the flunky but whenever Alfred wasn't busy in the kitchen he was at the mill learning how to pack shingles. In time he knew enough about the work he could get a job as a shingleweaver, a journeyman millhand. It paid good money for those times and it was a good trade in that area where the big Western Red Cedars hundreds of years old were just starting to be cut.

At the homestead we had wonderful neighbors; everybody helped each other. Uncle Will Broughton and Aunt Emma, who was Dad's sister, and their five children lived only a mile and a half from us. They moved from Illinois the year after we did. We had lots of fun with the kids.

Some of our other neighbors were the Breckenridges; Kelly Epson; Aaron and Kate Lewis and family; the Stillwells; Fred and Helena Sutter and their two children, Nellie and Fritz; Aaron and Ida Emery and their eight children, and Fred Neuenschwander, a bachelor. When any of the neighbors went to Port Angeles he would bring everyone's mail, and groceries too, if he knew what you wanted.

We bought an old white horse for twenty-five dollars. We named him Two Bits because of the price. When we had to pick up mail or groceries from some neighbor who had brought them from town for us, Francis would get on old Two Bits and go after it. When he was ready to start home Francis would put the mail and other items in two gunny sacks, connect the necks of the sacks with a short piece of rope and sling them over the saddle, one on each side.

That was easy, but balancing a bale of hay in front of him on that horse was a lot harder. We had no road yet, and when the crew put the trail in they just went around the stumps. There were a lot of stumps and a crook in the trail for each one.

By the time I was eleven years old we had acquired sheep, chickens, and two cows. Francis was working away from home so I had to learn to milk. Mama formed an egg tumor on her arm and it bothered her to make bread, so I learned that job too.

We had only three months of summer schooling that year. We walked three and a half miles to the Blue Mountain School—after our chores were done.

One of the bright spots of 1905 was a trip to Lake Sutherland, a fourteen-mile ride from town in a team-pulled wagon over rugged roads. the lake is about two miles long and less than a half-mile across and is kept filled by creeks running into it from the high, timbered hills rising straight up from its edge. There were only two places on its shore that were flat enough for a campground. The one we went to was, and still is, called Maple Grove. The lake was separated at its west end from a more popular and larger resort area, Lake Crescent, by a ridge but for some reason Mama picked Lake Sutherland for our week's vacation.

So one Saturday morning we packed the wagon with bedding, groceries, a tent, and our clothes and started for the lake. The route went along what became State Highway 112. The land was fairly level until we got out to where the road now turns south near Dry Creek Grange Hall.

There, some road builder must have decided the shortest way was the best way. Instead of working its way around and down the side of the hill to the Elwha River, the road went in a line ahead, past Al Eacrett's farm, through the woods and right over the edge of the hill and straight down to the river.

The road was steeper than a scared cat's spine. Even with the wagon's brake on it didn't help too much. It wasn't much of a brake. All I can remember is you pulled on on iron handle and that worked a brake shoe on both hind wheels.

Well, I thank God for my brother Alfred. I took a look at that road going down the hill and started crying and made it plain I wanted to get out of that wagon.

Mama told me to sit still. But Alfred said, "Whoa," to the horses and then said to me, "Jump off, Sis."

When we got down the hill, with them riding and me walking, and across the Elwha River bridge we were on our way to Eden Valley, a narrow strip of land that wound through the hills toward the lake. Some place on the valley road we turned south again and climbed up a long hill. Then we started down—and I mean *down*—to Lake Sutherland. It was worse than the road to the river.

God bless Alfred again. He looked down the hill, and without waiting for a single word from me he yelled, "Whoa," and said, "Jump off, Sis," and I did.

I think my sister Earline was a little scared, but she and Mama just looked at me standing on the ground, like I wasn't one of them, and rode down the hill to the lake.

We pitched our tent and that's where Mama and Earline and me slept and what we sat in when it rained. Alfred had to go back to work. We cooked outside over an open fire.

It seems to me there was a very pleasant man who was caretaker at Maple Grove. He rowed Mama and Earline around the lake in a boat but I got left out. The boat probably wasn't big enough for all of us. We girls fished and played house and had a good time.

The next Saturday Alfred came all the way out there again to bring us home. For some reason going up those hills wasn't as bad as going down.

An early Elwha bridge

Chapter 4

With animals added to the homestead, troubles came.

One night when I was twelve, Mama came to the bedroom shared by Earline and me. It was about midnight. Mama said she could hear Dan, a second horse we had bought, thumping around in the barn. We went out to see. When we got back to the house Earline and I told Mama that the horse was acting funny.

"Take the lantern and the dog and get Uncle Will," Mama told us.

We put our coats on and then got Shep. We tied two ropes around the dog's neck. That way one of us could walk on each side of him holding a rope. If Shep started to run into the woods on Earline's side, I pulled on my rope and if he went the other way, Earline pulled on her rope. It was black-dark; we were scared stiff. It was a mile and a half walk and Shep was our only protection.

We knew there were cougar in the area. They had been getting our sheep and when we carried water a quarter-mile in five-gallon buckets from Spit Creek to supply the house, sometimes we could hear a cougar's screaming cry. There were lots of bear around too.

But we knew the trail, and we met no wild animals. Uncle Will got right up when we called him. He found a long-necked bottle and put some kind of liquid in it, probably Watkin's Liniment, a remedy most homesteaders used, and we started for home.

Whatever he put in the bottle, Uncle Will added some warm milk and poured it down the horse's throat, using the neck of the bottle to get the mixture as far back as possible. By morning Dan was fine.

Shep was a typical farm dog. All the homesteaders had at least one. We did not have money for expensive canned dog food and the dogs slept outdoors. For their meals they had food scraps from the table which were put outdoors for the dogs to eat. We never had to give them a bath. They just rolled in wet grass and shook themselves dry.

They were good watchdogs and nice to have along when going out in the woods to look for cows. They were also company when picking berries or fishing. We kids loved the dogs and they in turn helped take care of us. It was a feeling of security to all the youngsters, and the parents too, to know the dogs were with the kids when they were playing or working out in the woods.

We had a pet sheep too. We called her Nanny. She would let me ride her, as long as we had a rope around her neck and Earline kept the other end looped around a peg in the ground. Earline was afraid to ride her. I don't know why we called her Nanny—that was usually a goat's name—but we did.

Cougars got most of our sheep but Nanny managed to fight one of the big cats off although she came home with her belly slashed open. She could hardly walk.

Alfred got some silk thread and told me to sit on Nanny's head to keep her down while he sewed her up. When he ran out of thread, he told me not to let Nanny up and he went to the house for more.

Gosh, talk about being scared. I could see a cougar jumping on Nanny and me at any moment from any direction.

A cougar

Francis, Earline, Mama, Emily, Alfred

In a couple minutes, Alfred came back with the thread and finished his sewing. Before long Nanny was ready for riding again.

Earline was skittish around the farm animals and that sometimes got her in trouble. If they got a chance, the rams would try to butt us. When Earline saw a ram coming she would panic and climb a tree. Sometimes being scared would make her climb so high I would have to help get her down.

My sister never learned to milk the cows but she would feed them their shorts, a form of ground grain, while the cows were in the stanchions. One day while I was milking she walked past me between two cows to get to their feed boxes. When she leaned way over to put the shorts in one cow's feed box, the cow alongside butted her on in, head first.

You never heard such yelling! I stopped milking and hollered, "Are you hurt bad?"

She was wiggling as hard as she could and her legs were waving in the air. "I don't know, but I'm coming out to see," she mumbled back as her face, plastered with the gray, powdery shorts, appeared.

Mama got enough money to buy two baby pigs from Hile Jacobs, a neighbor. Francis, who was so gentle with animals and people that Mama always said he should have been a doctor, rode to Hile's place to get them. It was a hot day.

Hile and Francis put each pig in a sack, tied the sacks together and hung them over the saddle, just like hauling groceries and mail. But when Francis arrived home one of the little pigs was dead. It had smothered. If he had only known to put some holes in the sack, Francis would have never let that happen.

Although he was good with animals, Francis wasn't much of a pig pen builder. The pen was made of split rails laid between upright posts. The pig just lifted a rail and came out, squealing and heading for freedom. Earline and I chased that pig every day. When one of us got on each side of it we would try to herd it back into the pen but that pig went every direction but that.

When Francis was there to help us, he made it look easy. Using that way he had with animals, all he had to do was call, "Come, piggie, pig, pig," and the so-and-so would go right into the pen for him!

It wasn't any wonder animals took to Francis. It was hard for any living thing to not like Francis. He was cheerful, had a great sense of humor, and could keep you entertained for hours with scary stories that would curl your hair. Everyone liked him—he could get acquainted with a person in ten minutes.

Francis was six-foot and weighed one hundred and sixty-five pounds—slim as a rail. No wonder the girls wanted him to teach them to dance.

Alfred was different. He was shy, wouldn't touch a drink, not that any of the family were drinkers. He was sober in nature too—serious. And so good to us kids. About five-foot, nine inches tall and average weight, Alfred wasn't a big man, but he was a worker. He was only sixteen when Dad left but he took over.

Mama relied on Alfred. He was the breadwinner.

We could get potatoes by going to other farms and digging them for a share of what we dug. We could do the same thing with fruit we picked so we needed a root cellar. Francis built one in the hillside near the house. It was lined with logs but it needed dirt on three sides for insulation, to keep the vegetables and fruit from freezing or getting too warm.

To move the dirt we used a slip scraper pulled by a horse. I drove the horse while Francis held the scraper. I was too small to control the horse, let alone make it go slower. I was on my stomach most of the time, but I never dropped the lines.

One day we went to play with Aunt Emma's four girls. She also had a boy. When we got there she had a new baby girl named Julia. Earline and I wanted to give the baby a present but we could not think of anything to make and there wasn't any money to buy a gift.

One day a lone wild goose flew down into our field. Francis grabbed his gun and shot it. When he was cleaning the big white bird I was watching and I said, "Save the windpipe. We can dry it and put pretty rocks in it for a rattle." We did and Julia played with it for a long time.

Guns were an important part of homesteading. They were necessary to protect our animals and ourselves from predators and to furnish venison and other meat. The stock on the farm was never enough to feed us.

We kids were scared of what the cougar and bears might do to us and we saw what they did to the farm animals. Although we were never attacked we heard stories of others who were, and walking through the woods was scary. We couldn't see very far into the brush and, gosh, what the noises would do to our imaginations. So we didn't feel bad about seeing wild animals killed.

Three of the Broughton girls walked over to our house one day after lunch. Alfred, who was one of the ambitious kind (even though he was on crutches after hurting his foot while cutting cedar bolts at the mill) said, "Let's all go for a walk." It was only one half mile to where we could look down at McDonnell Creek so we decided to go there. As everybody did in those days, we took a gun along.

When we got above the creek Alfred saw two young cub bears about half-way up a tree. He shot them both. Bears were one of the enemies in those days.

Francis ran down the hill and got the two cubs. About that time the mother bear, which was down by the creek, got wind of what had happened and started up the hill, bawling her rage.

Alfred told Mama, "You and the girls scoot for home!" Mama wouldn't leave the boys but she sent us girls running for home.

The old cabin that had been on the homestead when we moved there—the one with no windows, just a big front door—was the handiest place so we ran in there. But instead of closing the door after we got in we left it open and hid behind it, all five of us. We figured that if the bear saw the door open she would figure no one was in there but if it was closed she would break it down.

By firing at the bear and scaring her, Mama and the boys got away—and with Alfred on crutches. It was quite an experience.

When they got to the old homestead cabin and found us five girls standing behind the big door instead of shutting it, we sure got our "up and comings."

The boys skinned the cubs and stretched their hides on boards and later tanned the skins. Mama roasted the cub meat and I guess it was very good. I didn't eat any but Uncle Will and Aunt Emma and their family were invited over to help eat it.

That Christmas, under the tree were two large bundles with Earline's and my names on them. Mama had made us each a muff out of the cub hides and lined them with red silk. They were beautiful. I used mine a long time, even after I was married.

Chapter 5

Several things combined to make our home the dancing center of Blue Mountain—Mama's piano, a new road, and a tongue-and-groove lumber floor.

The road had only been built to within one and a half miles of our place so Mama's piano had been left at Sutters. It was oblong, large, and flat-topped like a baby grand but the top didn't lift up. There was no way to get it up that twisty trail.

At least there wouldn't have been if we hadn't got a lot more snow than usual one winter. Fred Sutter, with the help of Fred Neuenschwander, Frank Heibeson, and Harve Anderson, put the piano on a sled harnessed to a horse and brought it three miles to the Broughton home (that was the end of the road) then a mile and a half on the trail to our house.

The piano was heavy but the legs detached and that was some help. The trail was crooked where it wound around big stumps so the men had to lift it to shuffle it around the corners. The trail came down a hill across our field and up a hill to our house. I can see that piano, sled, horse, and men yet.

The horse bobbed into sight over the hill first, a dark blob on the white horizon; then the man behind him holding the reins. Finally, the sled with the black piano. It looked just like a hearse with a pallbearer on each side, pulling or pushing on the sled to force it around snowy stump obstacles as the men and piano made their way down the white hill and up the other side.

Taxes on the homestead had to be paid every three years. We needed a road and we were three years behind on the taxes. So the county commissioners said if Alfred and Francis would put in a road to our house it would be payment for the taxes. It was some job for the boys—their first experience with dynamite and a horse and scraper. But in 1904 the road passed inspection.

Two years later the road the boys built from the west would be joined by a road from the east, from Texas Valley located between Blue Mountain and Sequim. It was only about three miles from our house to Texas Valley and then fourteen miles more to town. That was much shorter than circling around to the northeast from

Road in early 1900s

Texas Valley then going west to town.

The valley was a beautiful natural area on Lost Mountain and was homesteaded mostly by people from Texas. Mr. and Mrs. John Machenheimer lived there. They had a large family—four boys and four girls—and their home was a big ranch where they kept a herd of milk cows. All people in Blue Mountain knew and liked the Machenheimers through the dances and picnics they had at their home, both when there was only a trail to the valley and after the road was built.

It was Mr. Machenheimer who wanted to put a road down Lost Mountain and across McDonnell Creek to our place. He tried for two years before he finally got a contract from the county to start construction, according to his only surviving daughter, Susie Machenheimer Maybee, who is 93 years old.

The county allowed the Machenheimers five hundred dollars to do the work and Mr. Machenheimer and his sons John, Henry, Fred, and Charles put in the road. It must have been an awful job, and I'm sure they didn't make any money building three miles of road in that hilly, wet country.

One night we all went over to Machenheimers' to dance and, of course, everybody took food. It wasn't potato chips and pop either. It was sandwiches, cake, pie, and coffee. The only thing they had for music that night was a wind-up phonograph and one record we could dance by. It seems to me it was *Listen to the Mocking Bird.* We played it over and over and over.

But the Machenheimer road was still in the future when dances started at our house. With the road that Francis and Alfred built, a piano, and the good solid floor on the finished forty-foot by twenty-foot room of the house not much more was needed for dancing at our house.

What else was needed was provided by Ansil Jackson, Sam Emory and Alfred who took turns playing violin, and by Mama and Mr. and Mrs. Sutter who played the piano. Harve Anderson and Sam could call square dances.

Before, dances had been at the school house but it was small and the floor wasn't as good as ours.

The neighbors, including kids, came to our house before it was too dark to see the way and brought whatever they had on hand to eat for the midnight supper. Everyone stayed until it was light enough to go home and do the chores. The bachelors—there were about six to eight of them—usually got there first, about dusk. They didn't have to get kids ready. They sat around and talked until the families got there.

The dances were held about every other Saturday night in the winter but less often in the summer when there was more work to do. Usually about forty people came and weather didn't make much difference in attendance. Everybody had wagons and sleds for transportation. The night was filled with schottiches, polkas, waltzes, two-steps, circle two-steps, and square dances (or quadrilles as we called them).

During the circle two-steps—a dance with all the couples in a circle and partners traded several times—Lawrence Cameron used to cut across the room instead of trading partners with the couple in front of him. A boy put a stop to that by slipping a piece of smelly limburger cheese in Lawrence's pocket. The same trick was used on a bachelor if he appeared to be dancing with a certain girl too often.

The kids danced too, often with the adults, until the children got so tired they fell asleep. Their beds were benches stacked two-high along the walls of the room, like a row of bunks. Parents woke the children up for the midnight supper and put them back to bed when their stomachs were full. One dance, I remember, it just happened nearly all the women brought onion sandwiches, and that was a strong smelling dance.

Fred Sutter (We called him Papa Sutter.) showed all us girls how to dance—waltzes always first, then two-steps. He also showed me how to play chords on the piano.

The second year we had dances at our place it was decided to have a masquerade party. They all came early. First, all the women went upstairs to dress and when they were through the men got into their costumes. Such a sight—homemade costumes, and masks made out of cloth with black paint for eyebrows and red paint for the mouth.

The women were all in costume and waiting downstairs for the men when my brother Francis, who was always being clever, came in to get dressed. He wanted to know which one was Mama and he couldn't tell, so he said, "I can't find my outfit." Of course Mama gave herself away by jumping up and pointing upstairs to where she had left his costume.

Putting limburger cheese in each others pockets wasn't the only joke the bachelors played on each other. They always seemed to be up to some prank. One of them ended his bachelorhood with the neighbors playing a joke on *him.*

Fred Neuenswander was married to Delia Williams, a teacher at Blue Mountain School, and the neighbors planned a shivaree after the ceremony. When the couple got to Neuenswander's log cabin, the shivaree party made loud noises on washboards and tin pans.

Olympic Peninsula bachelors start for home after a dance. Note man carrying his "good" shoes and lantern.

The newlyweds locked the door and put out the lamp so Fred Sutter humped over and Frank Hebisen got up on his back so Frank could climb onto the roof of the cabin and stuff gunny sacks down the stove pipe.

It didn't take Fred and Delia long to open the door and come out of that smoky cabin. In spite of the prank, Fred and Delia's marriage got off to a happy start. But at least one of the bachelors didn't fare so well.

While in Illinois a young man fell in love with a divorced woman who had a three-year-old daughter. He left Illinois and came to Port Angeles where he took up a homestead on the Blue Mountain Road. The bachelor built a small house and a shed. The shed joined the house and served as shelter for the cow.

About two years after he homesteaded, he received a letter from his Illinois sweetheart saying she and her daughter were coming to Port Angeles and she named the date they would arrive. The bachelor borrowed a horse and buggy and drove to Port Angeles to meet her.

In time two more girls were born and with three children it was darn hard to make ends meet. The couple started quarreling and gossip was that he beat her. As time passed they quarreled more and more. One day he beat her harder than ever before. It scared the little girls so they ran to get a neighbor man to come help their mother.

But when the girls got back with the neighbor, their father was stretched out and their mother had him tied up. And with a butcher knife she was starting at his feet to cut his pants off. Her destination with that knife wasn't for sure but there was some thought it might endanger future fatherhood.

When the neighbor told about it later, he said the farther up the pants leg she cut with the knife, the greener got the face of the man spraddled on the floor.

Things got worse between the couple so they went to Port Angeles to get a divorce. The lawyer asked them how long they had been married.

They said, ''We never married.''

''Well,'' the lawyer said, ''you can't get a divorce if you never married.''

So they got married.

But it didn't help much so they went to Port Angeles again and this time got a divorce. She got half the land and custody of two girls and moved to town. He stayed and lived on his part of the homestead.

Although our home replaced Blue Mountain School as the dance hall, the one-room school building became our center of education when I was eleven. Earline, who was ten, and I hadn't attended school except for a little more than a year when we first lived in Port Angeles.

The summer before the summer we attended the Blue Mountain School we had lived in Port Angeles and, since school in town was held during the winter and the Blue Mountain classes were during the summer, Earline and I missed school that year too.

That summer in town the boys had both found work at the Filion Mill and Lumber Company—Alfred as a shingle weaver and Francis as a knot sawyer—and in April we moved back into our old Pine Hill neighborhood, just a few blocks east of the mill.

We took our two cows to town with us; many of the

Filion Mill, Port Angeles

19

homes had barns like the place we moved to. Cows roaming free made many homeowners build stout fences to keep them out of the yards.

One visitor, asked about what he thought of Port Angeles at the time, said he thought it was a very good pasture.

I milked our cows and Earline and I sold the milk for ten cents a five-pound pail full.

When winter set in the family moved back to the ranch because the mill work slackened and the farm needed care through the bad weather. But missing so much school is what made it so hard for us when we finally began to go to school steady. We girls had forgotten a lot by that time.

For three months each weekday the next summer Earline and I walked the two and a half miles downhill through the woods and past our neighbors' farms to the Blue Mountain School.

The route through the timber was scary sometimes when the wind blew the rain through the trees and the tops swayed over in a gust, then sprang back when the wind let up. But in the open it was pleasant, meeting the other kids and seeing what the neighbors were doing.

One of the farms we passed was that of Ansil and Dan Jackson. They planted rows and rows of carrots one year. The rows were a lot longer than hoe handles too. But those carrots provided Earline and I and the Broughton girls with one of the finest Independence Days we had while at Blue Mountain.

We wanted some money for the big Fourth of July picnic we always had at the Blue Mountain Schoolhouse. We were paid twenty-five cents a day and our lunch for hoeing those carrots. But what fun the money bought on the Fourth!

Sometime before the big day which, along with Christmas, was the only real holiday we got, Uncle Will Broughton collected money from a group of bachelors in the area. (They were the only ones that had any money.) Uncle Will would go to town and buy ice, prizes, lemons for a barrel of lemonade, and fireworks.

The ice was used for making homemade ice cream; the prizes went to the winners of the baseball tournament, horseshoe pitching, and footraces; the lemonade went to quench thirsts brought on by all the games, and the fireworks were for thrills and noise.

The money we earned in the carrot field went mostly for ice cream and fireworks. When the day was over the bachelors got at least some of the money back they had loaned for the doings.

Early in the morning the residents of the Blue Mountain area would begin to arrive on foot and by horse and wagon, all with their specialty prepared for the potluck. They placed the hotdishes, salads, pies, and cakes (to be eaten outdoors later) in the shed behind the school. The kids made their purchases that would mean a regular bombardment of firecrackers all day.

The banging of the fireworks didn't do much damage to anybody, except maybe the nerves of some of the grownups. The only foolishness I remember was a time one of the dumber, or meaner—I don't know which—kids handed a firecracker to a boy that was

Blue Mountain School and class

nearly blind.

The hard-of-seeing boy always held what he was handed up close to his eyes so he could tell what it was. When he started to put the lit firecracker up to his eyes, I knocked it out of his hand.

Then I took care of the bully. That kid would give a thought before doing a stunt like that again. I kicked his shins from his eyeballs down.

On the other big holiday of the year, Christmas, I also came up with some money but not so much—and some candy, too much candy.

Because we had the big 20 by 40 front room, where we had dances, Mama and the Broughtons decided to have Christmas at our place. We kids found a nice Christmas tree, cut it down, and put it up in our front room.

We kids on the homestead only had candy on Christmas and ice cream on the Fourth of July and little or none in between. My oldest brother Alfred had gone to town and bought a big bag of hard candy and he hid it in among the Christmas trimmings we would be using to decorate with.

Well, my sister and I and the four Broughton girls trimmed the tree and ate all the candy Christmas Eve. Later that night we paid for stuffing ourselves with candy. We were busy as bees flying back and forth to a hive, just going back and forth to the outdoor biffy.

We had been taught to put the lantern light out when not using it. But if we had put out the light that night another one of us kids would just have to light it again in a couple of minutes when making another trip to the biffy.

To this day I can't remember if Mama let us have our

Christmas presents or not. That could have been our punishment. As the old saying goes—"Live and learn." And we learned.

Another Christmas, homesteaders in the area were invited to Aaron and Ida Emory's home for Christmas. They had eight children and a nice big log house, with a fireplace, located about half-way down Blue Mountain from our place.

Everybody was supposed to sing, tell a story or jig to music. One of the Emorys found out I knew the poem *Little Orphan Annie* by James Whitcomb Riley.

He asked me to recite it but I said, "No!" Then Sam offered me ten cents—which looked as big as a dollar to me—and I jumped up and said that poem:

Little Orphant Annie's come to our house to stay,
An' wash the cups and saucers up, an' brush the crumbs
  away,
An' shoo the chickens off the porch, an' dust the hearth,
  an' sweep,
An' make the fire, an' bake the bread, an' earn her
  board-an'-keep;
An' all us other children, when the supper things is done,
We set around the kitchen fire an' has the mostest fun
A-list'nin' to the witch-tales 'at Annie tells about,
An' the Gobble-uns 'at gits you
      Ef you
         Don't
            Watch
               Out!

Onc't there was a little boy wouldn't say his pray'rs—
An' when he went to bed at night, away up stairs,
His mammy heerd him holler, an' his daddy heerd him
  bawl,
An' when they turn't the kivvers down, he wasn't there
  at all!
An' they seeked him in the rafter-room, an' cubby-hole,
  an' press,
An' seeked him up the chimbly-flue, an' ever'wheres, I
  guess;
But all they ever found was thist his pants an'
  roundabout!

An' the Gobble-uns'll git you
      Ef you
         Don't
            Watch
               Out!

An' one time a little girl 'ud allus laugh an' grin,
An' make fun of ever' one, an' all her blood-an'-kin;
An' onc't when they was "company," an' ole folks was
  there,
She mocked 'em an' shocked 'em, an' said she didn't
  care!
An' thist as she kicked her heels, an' turn't to run an'
  hide,
They was two great big Black Things a-standin' by her
  side,
An' they snatched her through the ceilin' 'fore she
  knowed what she's about!
An' the Gobble-uns'll git you
      Ef you
         Don't
            Watch
               Out!

An' little Orphant Annie says, when the blaze is blue,
An' the lampwick sputters, an' the wind goes woo-oo!
An' you hear the crickets quit, an' the moon is gray,
An' the lightnin'-bugs in dew is all squenched away,—
You better mind yer parents, and yer teachers fond and
  dear,
An' churish them 'at loves you, an' dry the orphant's
  tear,
An' he'p the pore an' needy ones 'at clusters all about,
Er the Gobble-uns'll git you
      Ef you
         Don't
            Watch
               Out!

The moral of the stories about the Fourth of July and Christmas could be that even in the early 1900s money still talked.

Chapter 6

On each weekday of the summer, we walked down the gentle slope of the hill and the Blue Mountain School would be waiting there in the clearing with its ridged, ungabled roof and white-painted lumber sides.

We walked in the one door, hung our coats on the racks just inside and straightened our dresses on our way over to the tall cupboard along the right-hand wall. We opened the cabinet's large doors and placed our lunches on a shelf where they would stay until noon. The full-length locker was also where the blankets used by the kids, and the kettles used by their mothers, during social events were stored.

On the wall across the single room stood a table just big enough to hold the bucket and dipper for drinking water the pupils brought from a nearby creek.

The wall in the front of the room was the teacher's

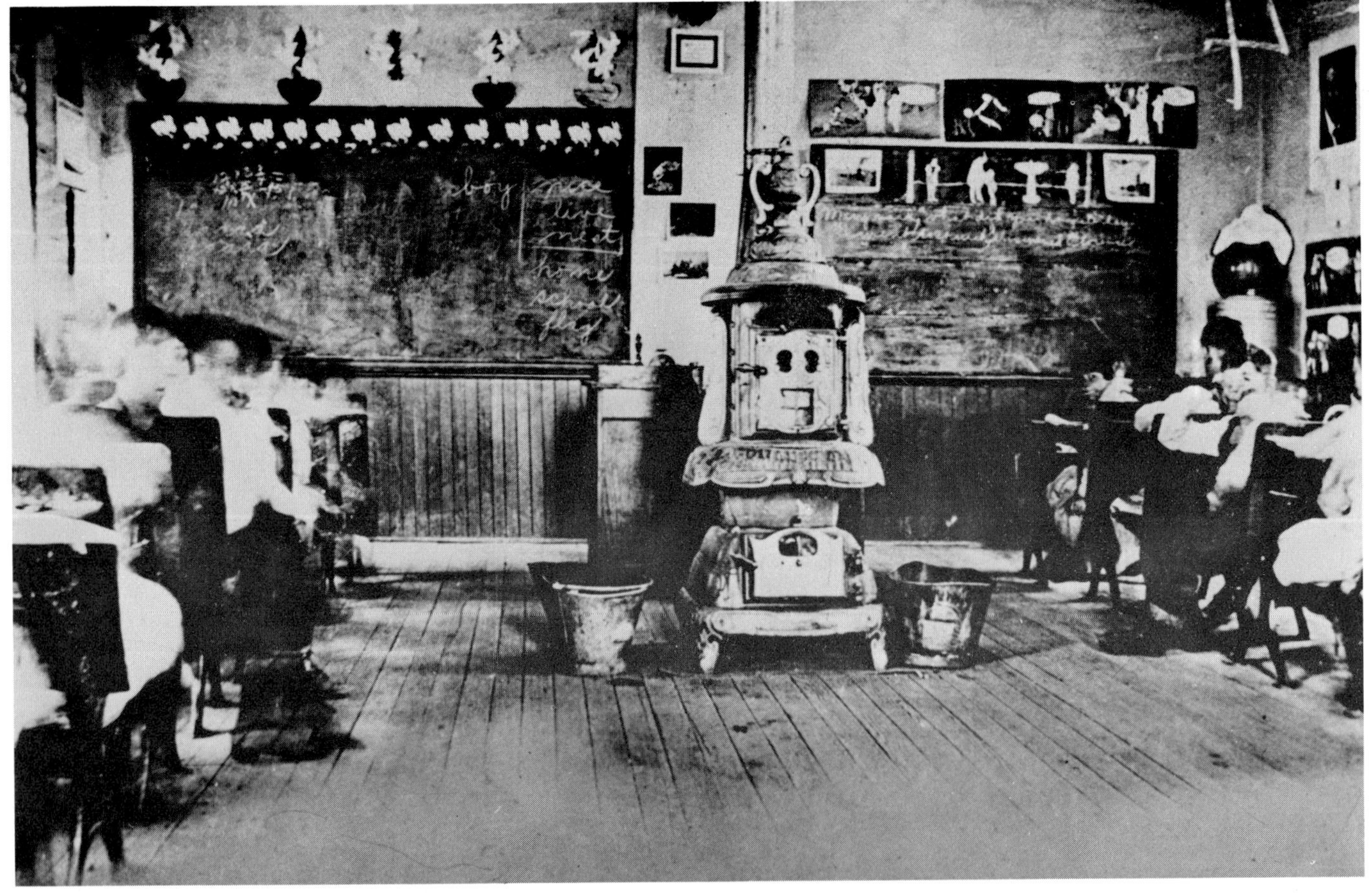

Blue Mountain School classroom arranged slightly different than when Emily attended

VanKuren School at Blue Mountain, 1906

place of business. Her desk dominated the left-hand corner and the blackboard stretched from there to the opposite wall.

An aisle led from the teacher's domain to the back of the room, through the two rows of double seats and desks. There was a question whether we dreaded that walk up the aisle when asked to recite or be corrected worse, or whether it was worse to watch the teacher come down the aisle toward us, with us wondering who was in for it this time.

The room could easily hold twenty-four pupils and it was nearly full. With its lumber construction, matched flooring, and its removable, manufactured seats and desks (that during socials were moved against the walls for children to sleep on) the building was quite modern for a frontier school.

The VanKuren School, two miles south, was more like a pioneer schoolhouse. It was there that in the year I was twelve I had the first full nine-month schooling since the last winter we had spent in Port Angeles.

It was about the same distance walking to the VanKuren School as it was to the Blue Mountain School but it was a lot wetter hike. We often had holes in our shoes because we couldn't afford new ones or get the old ones fixed. Mama's answer to that was four pieces of

cardboard a day. The cardboard was put in the bottom of the leaky shoe—one for the walk to school, one for each of the two recesses, and one for going home—but they didn't do much good.

The trail to the VanKuren School was over a series of rises and between each rise was a low area with lots of standing water. In one place I could walk a big fallen log but most of the way meant wet feet in the rain. Earline managed to get out of going over that watery trail. Mama was sick that winter and Earline had to stay home and care for her.

I was always scared going through the woods, but the worst place, especially now I was alone, was a tree where a man was found sitting with his back against the trunk, dead of a heart attack. And there was another place, where a man who suffered from epilepsy shot himself to death when he felt an attack coming on and feared he would be sent back to an asylum. It was hard not to run past those places, and often I did.

The VanKuren School was built of logs and had cracks in its split-cedar plank floor. When we dropped a pencil, we lost it; it went down through one of the cracks. So much dust raised from the rough flooring that when we swept it we had to wet it down to keep from choking.

The building, like the Blue Mountain School, was only

one room and had double seats and desks, but they were homemade of split cedar and nailed to the floor. Both schools had wood-burning stoves.

The walls of the VanKuren School were the same inside and out—logs. The ceiling was of split cedar. The teacher and the blackboard (a smaller one than at Blue Mountain School) were at the front of the room, opposite the door. Both buildings had windows along each side. The Blue Mountain windows were boarded up on one side when it was decided that light from both directions was not good for the pupils' eyes.

In the clearing outside the schools, during recess, the favorite game was Pump, Pump, Pull Away. Two teams lined up opposite each other with the kid who was "it" in the middle. "It" would call a team member's name and holler, "Pump, pump, pull away; come across or I'll pull you away."

The trick was to run across to the opposite team without "it" catching you. If you were caught while running across or you were pulled out of the team, you were "it."

Because we were in the high foothills of the Olympics, there was more snow than in the lower lands. During the worst of the snow I boarded at Walkers', about half-way to the VanKuren School. To pay for my board I did the cooking and other household chores and in the summer Mama gave piano lessons to the Walker girl once a week.

The VanKuren School was built when Jim VanKuren provided money for the materials and Omer Myers donated an acre of land. Neighbors used to say VanKuren furnished the money, Myers furnished the land, and Camerons furnished the students.

The Amos Camerons had fourteen children. The class was made up of Camerons, Walkers, and Bowers. About a dozen children were in the school the year I went there.

Bessie, who was the oldest Cameron daughter, brought the lunches for her brothers and sisters in school. It took a ten-pound pail to hold them all. And they always had big white sugar cookies, I remember.

The Bowers had eight children. It was quite a sight to see Bill Bowers' wife come down the road with her offspring. One of the smaller kids would be in a sack slung over the saddle and hanging on one side of the horse, and another in a sack on the opposite side. The older ones would be walking down the road behind the horse led by Mrs. Bowers.

There was very little work for men in the wintertime so in the fall Alfred would bring home canned goods, sugar, flour, four five-gallon cans of coal oil (kerosene), and three boxes of candles. When the lamps had used all the coal oil we used the candles for lighting. When the candles were getting low, Earline and I would split up cedar real fine. We would burn the cedar in the stove a piece at a time so Mama could sit in front of it on a pillow and read to us from the light the fire made. That way Mama, who was a wonderful reader, could still read every night from *Youth Companion*, the only paper or magazine we received.

We had deep-set window sills where Mama used to put the lamp the nights we still had coal oil. One night Earline and I came back from the creek, each with a five-gallon can of water, just after Mama had lit the lamp and put it too close to the window curtains and set the curtains on fire. All we girls could think of was Mama. We threw the ten gallons of water all over her instead of the fire.

She grabbed a rug off the floor and beat the fire out. Mama was small—five-foot, two inches tall and weighed 102 pounds—and when the excitement was over she looked like a scalded, white leghorn chicken ready to pluck.

Cameron Family and home, 1908

Chapter 7

Four special things happened the year I was thirteen—our well was dug, and a milkhouse, an outhouse, and a playhouse for my sister and me were built.

The well came first and the boys asked another homesteader, Harve Anderson, to help them dig it. Harve had lost almost all his hair and that tempted me into doing something that was almost my downfall.

The well was dug down about fifteen feet and we girls were lying on the ground at the opening looking down on Harve as he was digging, and at Harve's bald head shining down there. That was just too much for me, so I waited until he was right below me and I spit. It landed right on target.

I never knew a man could come out of a fifteen-foot hole so fast. He grabbed me and shook the daylights out of me, and demanded, "Don't you ever do that again!"

I never did. And I still have a great respect for bald heads.

Alfred and Francis were only home from work on Sundays so to make a milkhouse for me to put the milk into took quite a while. But when they were through it was nice and cool with its big, screened opening across the whole front of the north side of the six-foot by eight-foot building. We skimmed the milk there after the cream raised, then later churned the cream into good, yellow butter.

Next came a large outhouse. The old one had been built way too small, and the hole dug below it was no longer a hole—it had reached its capacity. As the outdoor privy was going up it made a fine playhouse for Earline and me. That might have given the boys an idea for what they did next. They started building a woodshed—at least that's what they said it was.

One Sunday after they started, Alfred said we girls could go fishing in McDonnell Creek, take our lunch and stay as long as we wanted to. That was a real treat. We didn't get to go to the creek very often although it was just on the east boundary of our land. There was too much work to do around the house; Mama was strict and we did what we were told to do. But once in a while,

especially when the Broughton girls came over, we were allowed to fish a pool below a falls where we caught lots of trout six to eight inches long.

A favorite spot: Emily at McDonnell Creek falls

When we came home in time to fix supper, here this "woodshed" had two windows, a door you could shut, two canvas cots, and a table with a pretty, little lamp on it. It was a wonderful surprise for us girls.

Summer could be a lively time around the homestead. We always had lots of company. But sometimes it was tough on Earline and me.

One time, when I was thirteen, our cousin Homer Huylar from Seattle came to visit and three girls from Port Angeles came out. Alfred, Francis, Homer, Mama, and the girls went to Deer Park near the top of Blue Mountain for a week.

With the milking, sheep to go find every night, and a garden to weed Earline and I had plenty to keep us from getting lonesome. But one evening, for some reason, we felt scared to stay alone so we walked a mile and a half over to Aunt Emma's to have our cousin Jeanette come stay all night. She was too busy so we asked Aunt Emma's next-door neighbor, May Elves, if she would come home with us and she said, "Sure."

That was the night I burned up the knife. When we got home I cut shavings from a piece of cedar—there were no newspapers available for starting fires in those days. I guess I left the knife in the stove after making shavings. Anyway, that's where I found the blade the next morning.

May Elves, who stayed with us that night, was our mail carrier for the short time we had rural delivery after the folks in the district got up a petition requesting it. Ella Kale was postmistress and had the post office in her home. She drove fourteen miles to Port Angeles to get the mail. The postmistress' pay was based on the amount of mail that was sent but the cancellation of so few letters was not enough to make the service pay.

I made pies the day the folks were to come home from the mountains. I used lard but the crusts weren't very flaky. But they ate the pie, with the help of a lot of whipped cream.

Packing by horse

It was the summer of 1908 and Miss Alice Johnson was our teacher at Blue Mountain. Many of our teachers were just high school girls who had gotten certificates to teach, but Miss Johnson had been to Normal School, the teachers' college of those days. She was good.

The first day school opened we all came into the schoolroom and sat in the double seats. Cecil Emory and I were in the same grade so we usually sat together. The first morning, Miss Johnson took her ruler, whacked it on the desk and said, "I am here to teach and I want your full attention when I talk to you!" She got it too.

If the other teachers didn't know how to teach fractions or some other part of a subject, they didn't, so when Miss Johnson came it was hard for her and hard for us.

It was that summer we taught our cousin Carl from Seattle that he should be careful about pulling tricks on people. Mama, Earline, and I were invited to Aunt Lillie and Uncle Charles Huylar's home in Seattle. It sure was a treat, except for one thing. Their son Carl, who was my age, took us kids for walks through the streets of the city then would run away from us, leaving Earline and I lost. Were we ever scared! Finally he would come get us and show us the way home.

When Aunt Lillie and Uncle Charles brought Carl with them to visit us that summer, Carl would go with us girls when we were looking for sheep. Carl had never been in the thick woods, and the salal brush on our place was thick! A person could walk on top of it easier than he could walk through it. There was only one other way—a log lying on the ground made a path, but it was hard to find. Earline and I would run away from Carl and cross the log without him seeing us. He sure hollered when he couldn't find it.

But what had been a fun summer didn't end that way.

Aunt Emma told us one day they had a book called *The Virginian* so Mama and us girls walked over to her house one afternoon to hear it read. The boys were clearing land down by the barn. Our cow was expecting most any day so before they walked over later for supper and to listen to Mama and Aunt Emma read the new book, the boys put the cow in the barn.

We kids lay on the floor while the two former school teachers took turns reading out loud by lamplight. For hours we were lost in the story about the handsome, drawling Wyoming cowpuncher transplanted from Virginia who was man enough to face down the villians with, "When you call me that, *smile."* And how we girls' hearts were swept away with the less than smooth path of his romance with the lovely Molly Wood.

It was four in the morning before the Virginian finally married Molly and author Owen Wister assured us the former ranch-hand had a long and successful life ahead of him—and we went home.

As we walked into our clearing we could see only smouldering ruins where the barn had been. The boys had set the slash-burning fires too close to the barn. The barn and our cow were destroyed.

The cow had tried hard to get out. Her horns were stuck deep into the wood that remained of the inside of the barn door.

Chapter 8

In the summer of 1909 we hiked to alpine meadows at Deer Park near the top of Blue Mountain. There was Alfred; Nat Broughton; Jeanette, his sister; Ada Kelly, my girl friend from Port Angeles; Charlie Lewis and his girl friend, Louise Whitmore; Grace Ross; Earline, and I. Uncle Will was our chaperone.

Two horses packed food and bedding and one horse, Old John, that belonged to Charlie Lewis, was brought along for the older girls Grace and Louise to take turns riding. I don't think there was anything Old John didn't do, or anyway tried to do. He was contrary and ornery. He and Grace turned out to be a darn good pair.

My brother Alfred always said, "Before you get married go to the mountains with your intended. That's where the true nature comes out." How true!

The first hint we had that the devil-horse recognized his sister was when Grace would grab hold of Old John's tail where the trail was steep without him kicking, ride him without him acting up, and she would tell him to whoa and he would stop. But poor Louise. When she would try to ride Old John he would either run or wouldn't go at all.

We had started about six in the morning. The trail was steep and about sixteen miles long, and it was a warm day. At one place, called the Devil's Backbone, the trail was nothing but loose shale and almost straight up. We had to claw our way up the Backbone and when we got there we little kids just flopped out on our stomachs. We made the whole trip to Deer Park that day.

After we caught our breath, we got a five-gallon oil can that was clean and built a fire to start cooking a spike buck deer Alfred had killed on the way up. It would be stew for the next day and following days. We found some wild onions to spice up the meat and vegetables. Alfred did most of the cooking.

When we unpacked the horses we found that a flour sack of currant biscuits Aunt Emma had baked and sent with us had turned into nothing but crumbs after being jostled around on the trail.

We had supper and Uncle Will was putting the blankets

Kids sliding at Deer Park are too fast for the camera.

down on the ground for our beds when we got another hint as to how Grace was going to behave. "Smell those quilts and don't give me one that was next to your old sweaty horse. I can't stand the horse smell," Grace demanded. So Uncle Will smelled the bedding and gave her the best.

The beds were arranged in a row along the hillside, with a space between where the line of girls ended and the boys began. Before we bedded down Alfred mixed the dough for slapjacks, just another word for pancakes.

We slept sound until about four in the morning. That's when Grace got up to her tricks again. She couldn't sleep so she got out of bed and filled a bottle with the slapjack batter, took a big spoon and dropped spoons full of batter on our faces. Gosh, we were mad!

It was just one thing after another. Grace didn't like to hike very much. She stayed in camp, ate all the cookies, and blamed us kids. It took us a while to get back at her, but we did.

There was a big snowbank on a hillside. We kids used it as a slide. All four of us girls—Ada, Jeannette, Earline, and I—put our legs up around the one in front and we held onto each other's legs like a toboggan and away we went. I was always in front. Fun! You can say that again! Our overalls were bleached out white. From the back we looked like albino deer.

Finally Grace wanted to slide down so she asked Uncle Will to cut a big branch off a tree for her to ride on so she wouldn't bleach her blue serge bloomers.

While she was getting ready for the slide, my cousin Jeannette and I came over and stood right beside her. Just when she squatted to plant her bloomers on the branch we pulled it away and she left without it. She couldn't stop from sliding all the way on her proud blue bloomers. The snow, and water at the bottom of the snowslide, sure did change the color of them.

But except for Grace the trip was pleasant. The weather was good the several days we were there. We took hikes during the days and sat around the campfire and sang songs and told stories at night.

Some boys at a nearby camp kept singing *Pretty Red Wing*, probably to attract us girls, but we never got to meet them.

Eight kids on a horse: Fritz and Nellie Sutter, Marie and Dot Broughton, Emily and Earline, Jeannette and Lara Broughton. Fred Sutter holds the horse.

Chapter 9

Well, here's a goodby to our homestead days. There were hard times and good times but we learned tolerance and a closeness to each other that over the years has never been broken.

Earline and I had two wonderful half-brothers. They were the bread winners of the family, even as teenagers, and always as kind, considerate, and helpful as any brothers could be.

In the summer of 1909, Alfred and Francis heard there was a mill for sale at Upper Elwha, a community of settlers along the Elwha River. Upper Elwha was west of Port Angeles. It was almost 30 miles by road from the homestead.

The mill was a double mill. There were two long buildings side by side, open to the weather on the ends, each with a roof like a wide-spread A. You could saw

Shingle weavers

Elwha Mill, 1910-1914

lumber out of logs under one roof, or run the other side to make shingles out of sixteen-inch-long chunks of cedar called blocks.

After the shingles were sawed from the block they dropped down from the elevated platform where the sawyer was to a man known as a knot sawyer who trimmed the shingles and cut the knots out. The work was very dangerous. Many of the "shingle-weavers" lost fingers to the saws.

Harry Coventon and Ed Isbell owned the mill. They got a contract to build a covered bridge across the Elwha River in 1909 and cut the lumber in the mill. When they heard the mill was for sale, my brothers came home all excited and wanted to buy it. Of course, we girls were never told anything. We were told what to do and that's what we did. Years later we found out they mortgaged the homestead to Ed Isbell to buy the mill.

The boys took over the mill in April 1910 and we moved to Port Angeles in August of the year before. By that time the forty-foot by forty-foot log homestead house had become very comfortable. A front room twenty by forty, a kitchen (Alfred built a chimney for the kitchen, lit a fire in it and it fell apart from the roof eave up so he mixed more mortar using more lime and built a new one that stayed), a bedroom for Mama downstairs, and then four bedrooms upstairs.

We had a stairway from the kitchen to the upstairs. The stairs were steep and had no railings. I couldn't even go up those stairs today. But at first it was even worse—we only had a ladder.

That ladder! It scares me yet just to think of it, especially coming down it in the mornings with a chamber pot of "gospel measure." The good old days, they say?

Even the barn had been rebuilt. Albert and Francis had cut some shakes and logs, and, typical of the times, the neighbors came over and helped build a new one.

Earline and I started school in town in September. Oh, what an experience that was! We walked into a schoolroom that was bigger than the whole Blue Mountain Schoolhouse—and we seventh graders were just in the annex. The higher grades were in the main Central School building where Alfred had gone to school when we first came to Port Angeles.

When we went to class, I asked Earline, "Where do we sit?"

She said simply, "The biggest and dumbest in the back, of course." And that is just where the teacher put us.

The assignment for the next day's arithmetic was usually put on the blackboard the day before. A lot of the kids had most of it worked before school was out. But I was nearsighted like my dad so I would have to wait until school was out and then sit in a front seat to copy down the problems.

Some of the teachers back at Blue Mountain had only taught what was easiest for them. One of those things was not fractions so when Earline and I started school in town the kids were rattling off fractions like a spelling bee, and we were lost. But I can still remember the first day's lesson—thirty-three and a third equals one-third.

Central School may have been big but, like big towns

compared with small ones, it wasn't as friendly. When we went to Deer Park that summer I had new shoes with hobnails in the soles, to make for easier climbing. After we got back Alfred said to leave the hobnails in; they would make the shoes last longer.

But kids are kids, as we all know, and city kids didn't come to school with hobnails in their shoes. They teased me and called me Hobnail Bill. I got so I was afraid to go to recess. One day I quit going to recess all together when I found my lunch gone and my lunch pail filled with angleworms.

The pleasant thing about Central School was our teacher, Mrs. Inez McNutt. She was wonderful to us girls.

In April, Mama, Earline, and the boys went to Upper Elwha where they lived in the mill cookshack while Alfred and Francis got the mill going. We had brought our cows into town again so I was left in town alone to milk the cows and sell the milk to our customers until school was out.

That was the biggest house I ever lived in. I never have and never will like to live alone!

Well, we all finally ended up at the Elwha and nobody could have moved into a nicer community. It had a new schoolhouse and nine families, counting us. Young people totaled thirty-two in all—the Ed Isabells' eight, the Tom Lauridsens' three, the Harry Coventons' six, the Bert Herricks' three, the Edgar McNamarras' four, the Soverugn Hansens' three, the Harve Andersons' one, and the four of us.

The Elwha Bunch: From left Emily, Edith Isbell, Louis Isbell, Earline, Percy Bork, Dorothy Coventon, Helen Isbell, Sam Lauridsen, Bill Coventon.

Chapter 10

Having the mill was new to us. The boys worked hard keeping it going and we girls worked hard too.

The mill crew was busy cutting lumber for the growing number of resorts being built at Lake Crescent, about seven miles to the west, and for repairing the Aldwell Dam downriver from us. It was built to generate electricity. When it was rebuilt it supplied power for as far away as the U.S. Naval Shipyard in Bremerton, about eighty miles.

The boys had their hands full. In addition to running the mill, Francis and Alfred built us a two-story house nearby.

As for us girls, in the summertime, for the noon meal, counting my brothers, there were twelve men to cook for. We not only cooked but we chopped the firewood and packed the water we used.

Aldwell Dam construction

The mill hands were hard workers and hearty eaters. To feed them we bought fresh vegetables from Coventons, lots of carrots. I scraped carrots by the hour. When we couldn't get them fresh we bought vegetables canned, such as corn and string beans, by the case. Canned tomatoes were a favorite, especially heated with butter and pieces of toast in them.

One of my jobs was baking bread. I baked sixteen loaves every other day.

Meat, potatoes, and gravy were in demand. Salads weren't, although we would put out fresh lettuce and tomatoes when we could get them.

A typical breakfast would include fried potatoes (usually recooked boiled potatoes from the day before), eggs, ham or bacon, hotcakes, and coffee. The hotcakes were cooked on two big griddles that covered the top of the wood cookstove. Sixteen could be cooked at one time, eight on each griddle.

Dinner, the large meal, was at noon. There would be meat (mostly roasted), vegetables, potatoes, gravy, bread, coffee, and—always—pie.

Only a few stayed for supper because those with homes close by would eat there. The men who stayed got mostly leftovers.

In the wintertime the men didn't log as much as in the summers because of the slowdown in lumber orders and the bad weather. Since there weren't so many men to feed we could get dinner started before going to school and then Mama finished cooking it for the crew.

We had elk meat a lot of times during the winter when the snow forced the elk down into our part of the valley to find food. Alfred and Francis were good hunters.

An oldtimer who lived by the covered bridge over the Elwha also killed elk. The difference, as we saw it, was that he was selling the meat but we hunted just for food. He got caught by the game warden. It sure made him mad! So he decided to take it out on my brothers. He sneaked around in the woods and saw Francis shoot an elk and then reported my brother to the game warden.

The boys must have got wind of what the oldtimer had done because they cleaned the elk, cut it up, and put it into flour sacks. Then they buried the meat in a big sawdust pile down by the mill.

The game warden came out to the mill and said he had been informed the boys had killed an elk that day. Francis, with his poker face, told him he was welcome to look around. So the warden did. When he got tired and couldn't think of anyplace else to look he sat down to rest and talk for a while, and then went on his way.

The place he picked to sit and rest was on the pile of sawdust, where the meat was hidden.

My work wasn't all in the kitchen. Between the house and the mill were logs that had to be scrambled over to get back and forth. When I complained to my brothers about the mess they said, ''Hook up the team and drag them out.'' So I did.

There was a lot of work, that's true, but there was a lot of fun too. We still had our dances every other Saturday night but at Upper Elwha they were in the school. The building is still used as a community clubhouse.

The Elwha mill house

For music, Harve Anderson, who had moved to the Elwha from Blue Mountain, played the mouth harp, Ed Isbell and Alfred played violins, and Mama chorded on the piano. I only played the piano by ear but I knew a lot of tunes so we got along fine. Mama gave piano lessons to kids at Elwha but never got around to teaching us girls. It's like the shoemaker who never had time to make shoes for his own children.

Ed Isbell could play the violin pretty well but played many of the pieces too slow and too long, especially the waltz *Over the Waves*. Art Coventon said to me, ''I've some sneeze powder in a jar. I'll drop some near Ed and he'll think he's getting a cold and will go home.''

It worked. When he sneezed, Mrs. Isbell came right over and said, ''Ed, we better go home. You're coming down with a cold.'' With Ed on his way home, the tempo of the dancing picked up.

We even had a masquerade dance, like at Blue Mountain. Everybody worked hard on costumes. The two McNamarra boys and Francis made theirs out of gunny sacks and went as Indians. Their headgear was beautiful, with feathers—some even hanging down their back. They took first prize too.

But later, when Mrs. McNamarra looked for her feather duster and could find only the handle—that was a different story!

It was at one of the dances that Charlie Lewis bought me my very first bottle of pop. It was an orange soda. My first bottle of pop and I was sixteen years old. Now they start drinking pop at sixteen months. Charlie seemed to go where Francis and Alfred went. When we moved to Elwha he came along to work in the mill.

Charlie was six feet, two inches tall and slim—one hundred and seventy pounds. His hair was light brown and wavy. His face was long and slim—handsome with the exception of a nose that was a little too big. His greenish-blue eyes could reveal stolid stubbornness, humor, or all those feelings in between—affection,

Charlie and brother Alfred

gunny sacks. We pulled them tight around our legs with strings, the closest thing we could get to the new style.

We walked—or hobbled—along to the Herrick's little country store about three-quarters of a mile away. Along the way, near the store, there was a big old white fir tree surrounded by brush. Just as we got there dusk had turned almost completely dark.

We heard a noise in the brush and then a bellow. We thought it was Herricks' mean old bull.

We tried to run but got tripped up in the sack-skirts. We fell down. We rolled. We hollered. We made more noises than two cats fighting on a tin roof.

Then Charlie and my brother Francis came out of the brush laughing so hard they could hardly walk. They had taken a short-cut through the woods after we left and beaten us down to the spot. It was Charlie who could bellow just like a bull.

On Saturday nights there weren't dances the families got together and played Whist, a favorite card game. The

anger, determination, playfulness, tolerance—and occasionally a surprising depth of understanding.

He was not afraid of hard work nor was he scared to take a chance to gain a little in life. That last fact had a tendency to get him in trouble. Charlie had a practical joke side to him too.

Hobble skirts came in style. We knew we couldn't afford them so one evening Dorothy Coventon, Earline, **Dot Broughton** (who was visiting us) and I slipped into

Elwha School teacher, Miss Aldine Gilbert, loved to put on programs at the school house. (My sister Earline sure could sing, and I sang alto with her.) We had many picnics and hikes on Sundays.

Edwin Champion worked at the mill. One winter, in between lumber and shingle orders, he built a rowboat which we took to Lake Sutherland many times. Hay would be put in the bottom of the wagon used at the mill for hauling shingles. Coventons' team and our team of

Herricks' store on the Elwha

Log hotel at Lake Sutherland in early days of Maple Grove Resort

horses were hooked up and the four horses would pull a bunch of us out to the lake.

There was a time a hay ride to the lake didn't work out too well. Sam Lauridsen was taking a load of hay out to a farmer at the lake. He asked Cyrus and Goldie McNamarra, Earline, Dot and Art Coventon, Francis, and me to go along. All of us got up on top of the load, as high as the ridge of a one-story house. We had to go a mile on even rougher than usual road before we got to the main road to the lake.

Sam was driving and hit a big chuckhole. Lucky for us a tall fir tree was close. The hay tipped off the wagon but the tree caught the load before it went all the way to the ground. But the hay tilted far enough that we all slid off.

I was first to hit the ground and Cy landed on top of me. I had a big-rimmed hat on. When Cy hit me he knocked the rim off and down around my shoulders and popped every button off my shoes.

What a mess! We all helped put the hay back on the wagon but Sam wasn't going to take another chance at losing the load. Earline was the only one that got to go to the lake.

Sometimes we walked across the covered bridge to the Lester Sweets' place. Behind the house, in the woods against the hill, was an abandoned shaft called the Madison Mine. It was only a black hole in the ground just big enough to crawl into. There was nothing much to do in there except get covered with cobwebs but it was fun.

Other times we would hike to Baldy, a bare mountain of rock upriver from our home. On the way up the mountain a narrow passage between two rocks kept us from having to walk a long way around.

During one of the hikes we had a girl visitor with us who was two ax handles and a chaw of tobacco wide. We almost wore the hide off of her yanking and pulling her through. But nobody wanted to go to the top the long way.

Chapter 11

When I started in the eighth grade I went to school at Central in town although there was a school at Elwha. I don't know why. I just did what I was told. Because I had missed so much school I was sixteen.

I had to work for my room and board so I stayed with a school teacher we will call Mr. Smith and his wife. She was pregnant. I slept on a cot in their front room and did housework.

Mr. Smith always called me when he got up in the mornings so I could get breakfast. One morning he woke me up by touch—not by call. When I got back from school that night I packed my clothes and left. I had been there about three months.

I sure didn't know where to go, but Will and Mary Lewis and their three young boys lived up near Eunice Street. I had stayed with the boys two weeks that summer while Mary was in Seattle to be with her husband who was working there.

So I walked up to the Lewises'. Will was still working in Seattle. Mary said I could help around the house and she and I got along fine. I loved it there, but I had to leave when Will moved back from Seattle. He said Mary didn't need help—which she really didn't.

I moved in with Frank Lawrence and his wife, who we all called Aunt Carrie. It was swell while it lasted but they had three daughters and didn't need more help, so they

Old Central School

didn't need me.

I heard Mr. and Mrs. Jim Van Kuren who took in boarders needed help. They lived up on Tumwater Hill and were providing board for two teachers and a girl who worked at the cannery. With no bridges over the valleys in those days it was a long walk up and down hills the two miles to Central School.

I worked pretty hard there. I was up by five o'clock every morning. The washing for the boarders was done three times a week before going to school. Ironing was done three mornings a week.

Washing clothes meant boiling the white things in a tub on top of the cookstove and scouring each soapy piece of clothing against the metal corrugations of a scrubboard. It was hard on the clothes and the scrubber's back but it got the clothes clean.

When it came to ironing, a solid piece of metal shaped like today's electric irons was placed on the stove until it got hot enough to straighten out the wrinkles in the clothes but not hot enough to burn them easily if the iron was kept moving.

The Van Kurens had the type of carpet sweeper that had rollers with brushes on them. When the sweeper was pushed the brushes went around and picked up the dirt, but not all of it. So their rug, that covered the front room floor, was untacked each spring, hung outside and hit with a flat, stiff wire beater until the clouds of dust quit flying from it, then tacked down again.

The reason I got up at five each morning was to build a fire in the cookstove and cook breakfast. I had to get most the other meals too. When the dishes were washed at night it was usually time to go to bed.

The Van Kurens never had any children of their own, and I was sure lucky Mr. Van liked me. He always called me Jim. That was because I filled the spot of the son he never had.

Mr. Van had been in the Civil War between the states and was a member of the Grand Army of the Republic. After I had been there for quite a while he told me of his experiences in the war. One of them was about losing his leg.

While fighting he was shot just below the knee, he said, and was taken a prisoner and sent to Libby Prison in the South where he found a lot of his comrades already there. Nothing was done for his terrible wound, according to Mr. Van. It sounds awful, but he told me the flies on his leg left maggots that ate on the wound and kept the dreaded gangrene from setting in.

The Opera House

37

An Elks Lodge group on the stage of the Opera House.

For food, wheelbarrows of corn meal were brought in and dumped out on the ground to eat. The dead, Mr. Van said, were put in the same wheelbarrows and taken away.

There was a big yard out in front of the buildings. It was enclosed by high walls and guards were sitting up there on platforms to watch the Northern soldiers. A nice stream of water ran through the enclosure, but any prisoner starting for a drink was told he would be shot if he went on, was what Mr. Van told me.

Mr. Van couldn't walk with the half shot-off leg so he said he crawled over toward the stream. They yelled at him to stop or they would shoot.

Mr. Van said, "Go ahead. I'm dying anyway." They didn't shoot so he washed out the wound and crawled back to the prison, got a knife, and cut his own leg off—what was left of it.

Twice a month—every other Saturday night after work—I got to go home and stay until Sunday evening. Usually Alfred would take me back and forth. And I made sure that the Saturday nights I went home were dance nights at Elwha.

Sundays, when I wasn't at Elwha, we went to church—in the same building that is now the Angeles Grange Hall.

I slept with Mrs. Van Kuren in a feather bed. She was real small and there was plenty of room in the bed. By hitting the fluffy mattress on each side, in the spots where we each slept, the feathers would puff up in the middle and it was like two separate mattresses.

My schooling and working was about to end for that year. During my stay with the Van Kurens I became sick. Mrs. Van Kuren gave me a shot of whisky and told me to take a hot bath. I fainted in the bath and broke out with

Earline and Emily, right, in Eighth Grade graduation dresses

measles.

She phoned Alfred and told him to come get me. He came from the Upper Elwha with our horse and open buggy in winter weather. After that ride home the measles "went in," a complication making the disease worse.

I lost my hair and was one sick girl but eventually came out of it and grew new hair. I also gave the measles to my brother Francis and he never did forgive me.

The measles also meant I had to take the eighth grade over and I ended up graduating with Earline.

When we graduated from the eighth grade all country and city children went through the ceremony at the Old Opera House in Port Angeles on Front Street between Lincoln and Laurel Streets.

Earline had a white dress; I didn't. So the Elwha teacher Miss Gilbert, who boarded with us, loaned me one. We put hay in the big wagon to cushion the bumps and placed boards on the hay to sit on. Earline, Francis, Sam Lauridsen, Dorothy and Art Coventon, Goldie McNamarra and I all got into the wagon and started off for Port Angeles. Only Earline and I were graduating. The rest were just friends.

The graduation started at eight in the evening so we left the Elwha, twelve miles from town, at four. We had only blankets covering our knees to protect us from the cold. It was fun though. We took sandwiches and cake with us. No money to splurge buying lunches in those days.

There were lots of people in the audience of the big, high-ceilinged hall used for shows and other community events. Some school official gave a speech and Lucy MacKechnie recited while a mother rocked a baby in a buggy to keep it quiet. She wasn't very successful.

There was some singing then we all stood up in a line on the stage while the school officials handed our diplomas to us.

We got home after midnight.

Front and Laurel Streets, Port Angeles, 1906

Chapter 12

The summers of 1912 and 1913 were times of fun and romance.

The first year, the Elwha Bunch went to Idaho Camp. Alfred had told me, "If you can get Uncle Frank Broughton to come over from Blue Mountain and take care of things here at the mill we, and whoever wants to go, will spend a few days at Idaho Camp on Hurricane Mountain."

The area, now more commonly called Hurricane Ridge, is west of Deer Park where we had camped before. Idaho Camp was just a few yards below and south of the present southend picnic grounds at Hurricane Ridge. It was one of only two places on the mountain that had water.

Goldie McNamarra and I said we would ride out to see Uncle Frank. Goldie's family had a riding horse but we didn't so I borrowed one. We started early in the morning. It was twenty-eight miles—a long ride even for young girls. To make it worse we had heard before we started to Uncle Frank's that on Saturday, the week before, a man who worked in a logging camp some distance away and couldn't get home very often came home when he wasn't expected to and found a man visiting his wife.

The logger grabbed a gun and shot, but missed the man. And here it was Saturday night again as we neared the end of the trip and we were riding up a steep hill and had to pass this house.

Believe me, we tried to make those poor tired horses go faster even if it was steep! We could just see that logger taking aim at us, maybe thinking it was his wife's visitor coming back.

When cars first came on the market, it's true, if a car could make it up to the top of Blue Mountain Road it was sure to be sold. It was that steep. After going sixteen miles to Port Angeles from Elwha then on out to Blue Mountain and up those awful hills it was sure hard on those horses.

When we got to Broughtons' Uncle Frank said, "Sure I'll come out next week." We stayed all night and Uncle Frank had our horses saddled up and ready next morning. We only got as far as Morse Creek, a little less than half-way home, when my horse began to limp. I got off and we looked all over the horse and finally found out Uncle Frank had forgotten to put the saddle blanket on. The horse's back was sore.

Goldie and I took turns riding her horse and leading my poor thing. When we were out by Dry Creek, with about seven miles more to go before we got home, my brother Francis came by on his way home to Elwha with a wagon full of groceries and feed. Boy, were we tickled to see him! We tied the horses behind and rode home in the wagon.

Goldie McNamarra takes a break.

The Elwha Bunch play mock croquet

Hurricane Mountain was a lot like Deer Park, with small, scrubby evergreen trees, meadows with flowers and surrounded by snowy mountain peaks. It was where the trees ended and the rock mountains began.

By the time we were ready to go to Idaho Camp there was sixteen of us in the group and four horses packed with bedding, food and clothes—clear up to their ears. In those days horses were supposed to do the toting, not the people. Backpacks were used only if a person didn't have a horse or he was going where a horse couldn't go.

On the trip were Aldine Gilbert, our teacher; Charlie Lewis; Lella Constance; Alfred and Francis; Cy, Guy, and Goldie McNamarra; Sam Lauridsen; Harve, Anna, and Floyd Anderson; Dorothy Broughton; Mama, and Earline and me.

The trip was one of the highlights of my life. We took long walks every day—up Mount Angeles and out to Obstruction Point—and then back to camp where Mama and Mrs. Anderson, who were our chaperones, were waiting for us. Only, we teenagers didn't call them chaperones; we called them gooseberries, maybe because we considered them sour like the berries.

Mrs. Anderson wore a long calico dress and a long starched white apron. She was always holding up the edges of the apron and looking at it to see if it had gotten damaged.

Most of us kids dressed in more rugged clothes. Earline and Dorothy wore bib overalls like the boys but I was too chunky for men's overalls to fit. I had to wear an old dress. Lella also wore a dress, but it was too tight. It was a nightly job to sew up rips where the dress couldn't stand the strain and had split open during the day.

In the evenings Guy McNamarra would write plays. He would give us parts written out on slips of paper and we would act them out. It sure was fun!

We slept in a line as usual, with the boys on one side and girls on the other. There were always mice running around at night looking for food, and then maybe a warm spot for a nap.

They seem to favor Mrs. Anderson. Every night she would let out a holler each time a mouse would run into the foot of her blankets and scramble up to the top where he would jump out and run for his life at the commotion he caused.

Out of the young people on that outing, summer romances for four couples would grow into engagements by the next year. But one of the romances didn't work out even though Sam Lauridsen pulled a trick on us to woo my sister.

When we broke camp, Alfred said to Sam, "You know the shortcut down the ridge that will take you to the main trail to go home on." So Sam and four of us girls started down the shortcut, all right, but how and when I don't know, three of us girls found we were by ourselves. Earline and Sam were nowhere around.

But you can't get lost going downhill and we all got home safely—and being nice girls nothing was said to Mama.

Earline didn't become engaged to Sam but she did to Guy McNamarra. The other couples engaged by the summer of 1913 were Alfred and Aldine, the teacher; Francis, and Goldie, and Charlie and I. Charlie was twenty-eight and I was nineteen.

That summer we all went to Olympic Hot Springs. What a beautiful place for four couples in love—even if they did have a gooseberry on hand. This time the chaperone was Mary Lewis who later became my sister-in-law.

The hot springs were in a valley, almost a canyon, with steep hillsides covered with giant timber rising all around. Boulder Creek cut through the bottom of the valley and supplied fresh water to the rustic resort. The mineral waters came from small springs in a hillside. Boulder Creek ran into the Elwha River a ways upriver from our home.

Mama and Mrs. McNamarra were already up at the hot springs, probably trying to improve Mama's health which never seemed to be good, so Alfred said, "We'll shut the mill down and we'll all go."

We walked the twelve miles up there. Three horses packed our spare clothes, bedding, and food.

At the springs, the boys stayed in one cabin and we girls, with Mary, were in another. The cabins were more like tents, with wooden floors and sides, and pyramid-

Guy McNamarra rests during Elwha Bunch hike.

Bathing in Olympic Hot Springs, 1914

shaped tents on top. Because of the noises we girls made, the boys named our cabin Camp de Scream, and made a sign for it saying so.

We all took long walks during the days. One day we took a lunch and hiked to Boulder Lake, about three miles. Then another day we went to Happy Lake where we almost got eaten by mosquitoes. It was about twice as far as Boulder Lake.

Francis and Goldie rested on the way home from Happy Lake. It was warm so Francis took off his coat and forgot to pick it up when he got back on the trail. I guess he was still thinking about the coat when we were back at the cabin eating supper. Francis did something that was not polite and Goldie asked him, ''Where are your manners?'' Without thinking Francis answered, ''I left it up on the trail under a tree.'' We sure razzed him.

Meals were served in a big tent furnished with tables and benches. Margaret Everett, who with her husband Billy and her brother Carl Schoeffel ran the resort, did the cooking. We couldn't afford to buy meals so we cooked in our cabins but we went over to the big tent at night to listen to a man play a violin and to sing.

We enjoyed the pool. It was real primitive. Just a hole dug out and filled with hot mineral water. One end had smooth logs running down into the pool and I remember hanging onto a log at the top and then letting go and sliding into the water.

Although we wore swimming suits, only all men or all women could be in the pool at any one time. If the women were in the pool a white shirt was hung on a limb. A red shirt was hung out for the men. Not like it is today—where men and women can go in together, and maybe no clothes at all.

For people who didn't want to go up to the pool, two cedar logs and been hewed out for tubs. The water was very warm in them.

Most nights the boys would come over to our cabin. We would play Whist, and Mary kept a close watch on us. One night Charlie asked me to go for a walk with him. Our gooseberry spoke up and said, ''You better not, Emily. Your mother comes over here early every morning and looks at your shoes to see if there's mud on them.'' So you bet I didn't go.

Chapter 13

Our vacation at the hot springs ended and school started. Alfred thought Earline and I should go to school in town so it was up to us girls to find a place to work for our room and board.

I was lucky. I lived with Mr. and Mrs. Ed Fitzhenry on Laurel Street. They only had one child, Phyllis, eight years old, and while I worked for them Mrs. Fitzhenry discovered how nearsighted I was. She immediately told me, ''That holds you back in school work and it's not necessary. Saturday we'll go to town and get you a pair of glasses.''

It was wonderful to see the stars, blades of grass, and leaves on the trees. Before, everything in the distance was just a blur of color. Mrs. Fitzhenry sent the bill to Mama at the Elwha and I heard nothing more about it.

For a change good fortune was mine but Earline was having a bad time. She had problems at the places she worked and moved three times in three months. She finally quit school, without Mama knowing it, and went out to Blue Mountain to stay with Aunt Emma Broughton. Earline was independent and most people hiring houseworkers didn't admire independence.

Earline said to me when she quit school, ''Don't tell Mama.'' She—and I—were lucky; Mama never asked me how Earline was doing.

As usual, Earline landed on her feet. After two weeks with Aunt Emma, she found a job at $15 per month, an unbelievable amount in those days, doing housework for Mrs. Susan F. Phelps who had a drygoods business on Front Street two stores east of the Opera House.

To make a long story short, I was having an awful time in high school. One of my teachers, a man who tried very hard to help me, said, ''Your trouble is that you have no school foundation.'' That was very true. Our schooling

From left: Earline, Emily, Alfred, and Louis Isbell prepare for some bicycling while Mama watches.

had been broken up and many subjects weren't offered in the small schools we attended. I was nineteen and only a freshman in high school.

But Superintendent R. J. White thought I should stay in spite of my background. When I told him I was quitting school he said, "It isn't so much what you know that will count, it's your high school diploma that will get you a job." But I left, anyway.

That was 1913. My oldest brother Alfred married Miss Gilbert, the Elwha school teacher, on October 1 and moved the part of the mill that cut lumber to Blue Mountain. Timber couldn't be brought far to a mill if there was no railroad. Logging was near the mill at Blue Mountain. Besides, Alfred may have been homesick and he could still live at the old homestead. The mortgage had not been foreclosed yet.

Mama moved into town to a home we owned at Fourteenth and Cedar Streets. Before we moved to Elwha, Alfred had bought the four lots in town and started to build a barn that turned into a house.

Earline was no longer working for the drygoods store owner. She and Francis were living at Elwha where Francis ran the shingle mill.

I went to work at the Port Angeles Telephone & Telegraph Company for Frank Dustman, a fine man, and stayed with Mama. She was still pretty provoked with me for quitting school so no conversation went on when I got **home** from work. With her pride in her advanced education, she could never understand one of her daughters quitting school. She didn't seem to realize that being kept out of school so much had something to do with it.

When I started on the job I didn't have a set schedule. Many nights it was midnight or later when I got home after the fifteen-block walk. I was scared going home then, but nothing like I would be today!

I got along fine on the job and liked it very much. Remembering numbers was one thing I was good at and that was a big part of the work. The switchboard had a hole for each telephone line, and a light. When a light would flash, the operator would plug a jack into the hole and ask what number the person wanted to talk to. Then the operator would connect the two lines by plugging a jack into the line of the phone being called, and pull a lever that rang the number of short or long rings assigned to the person being telephoned.

My job ended when Mama went to stay with her sister on Vashon Island. During the three-month training period at the phone company, operators didn't receive any wages so when Mama left it was a matter of if one is to eat, one must work—and for wages.

So I quit the telephone company, something I have always regretted, and found a job with Mr. and Mrs. Al Jensen for five dollars a month, and room and board, of course. She entertained a lot so I earned every bit of my five dollars.

Frank Dustman and operators at the switchboard of the Port Angeles and Telegraph Company.

Aaron and Kate Lewis on their farm

Francis and the McNamarra boys had started logging and Earline went to work at the Elwha for Mr. and Mrs. Bert Herrick who ran a store and a pack train of horses to Olympic Hot Springs.

Well, that was goodby to the best times I ever had as a girl. Work? Yes! But every Saturday there was either a dance or a Whist party, all holidays were celebrated camping or hunting, and close friendships with the Elwha Bunch lasted for years.

As far as being popular, I wasn't—three boy friends as a girl. But my sister was popular and when she turned a suitor down he often came to me for comfort and sometimes took me out. I frequently found companionship with older people. I loved them and they liked me.

And there was Charlie Lewis, the man I was engaged to. He had moved back to Blue Mountain to take over the Lewis Homestead after his father deeded forty acres to him. Charlie had six cows to milk, the cream had to be separated, there were the calves to feed, and the rest of the hard work of a farm to do.

When Charlie courted me after he moved to Blue Mountain he rode his bicycle into Port Angeles to see me. Coming into town was not so hard for him. It was more downhill than up, but going back home was something else.

There were no high bridges across Ennis and Seibert Creeks yet. That meant pedaling all the way up out of each steep creek valley. The same situation existed at Morse Creek. And there were four hills to go over after he started up Blue Mountain.

Now Charlie had a home, more work than he could handle, and a fiance when what he needed was a wife. He wanted to get married. We set the date for June 27, 1914.

Aaron Lewis, who was Charlie's dad, Charlie's married sister Iva Myers and her husband Omer and two children Alvin and Lucy had come from Illinois in 1895. Both families took up homesteads on Blue Mountain Road.

Mother Lewis (Kate) and the two youngest boys of the family of ten children, who were all still at home, stayed in Illinois. It was two years before Mother Lewis and the boys could earn enough money to come out West. She sold butter, cottage cheese and garden vegetables, and at last the cows, to get the money for the trip.

About a year before Charlie and I were married Dad Lewis deeded the forty acres of land that had the house, barn and cleared land on it to Charlie. It also had a mortgage on it.

I had always said that when I did get married I wanted it to be at our family's homestead where Earline, Alfred, Francis and I had spent much of our childhood. I was lucky. Mama had moved to our Blue Mountain home to stay with Alfred and Aldine, so that's where the wedding would be.

The forty-by-twenty-foot combined dining room and front room provided lots of space. The neighbors brought flowers and helped make it look very pretty. An arch decorated with roses and other flowers was part of the altar.

And this time I had my own white dress. I bought it with money I earned at Jensens'. I didn't have to borrow one like at my graduation. The only trouble was that the princess underskirt I ordered was too full for the dress and it did two things—push the dress out and crowd in between my legs so it made it difficult for me to dance, but I was a good dancer and I didn't do too badly.

It did make Charlie unhappy. He didn't dance very well, anyway, but with the underskirt pushing my dress out, it got between his legs too.

I was so pleased, and still am, that five families drove that twenty-eight miles from Elwha to our wedding with either horse and buggy or team and wagon. Francis used his team and wagon to bring Guy, Goldie, and Cy McNamarra and their mother and Earline.

They started real early so they could help with preparations for the wedding, but on their way a back wheel of the wagon began to squeal. Francis had forgotten to bring a can of axle grease and the wheel began to get pretty hot. Mrs. Mac, as we called her, found the solution. She had two two-quart jars of meat to make meatloaf with. She took the lids off, scraped off the fat that had collected at the top of the jars, and greased the wheel with it.

Nobody had been able to bring Charlie's mother out from Port Angeles. There had been cars for hire in town for several years so Charlie paid five dollars to have one bring his mother to the wedding.

We were married by Rev. C. E. Fulmer of the First Methodist Episcopal Church, which cost five dollars. With the five dollars spent to have Charlie's mother brought from town, we had one dollar to live on until the next cream check came.

The Good Old Days!

Early road and cars

Chapter 14

We left our wedding reception at two in the morning. The violin and piano were still doing their best and so were the guests. Charlie and I walked the two and a half miles to the former Lewis place that was now our farm. It was dark but the trail was familiar. Soon the house and outbuildings became forms in the night and we were home.

Suddenly life was different. Most wives go through it, and husbands too. The married man or woman is not the same as the courting one. Charlie now became more dominating, courser, and my passive nature kept me from standing up to him.

I had been used to turning to gentle Alfred with my troubles. Now it was to Charlie, and his ear wasn't so sympathetic. I wasn't used to that. But in spite of whatever faults we had, our marriage worked. We cared for each other deeply. That and our other good qualities carried us through.

And much of my life didn't change. I had done farm chores as a girl on our homestead and, later, housework to earn room and board. I just put to work what I had learned.

We raised a lot of our food and got supplies from town once a week. We had one horse and a wagon. Uncle Will, who lived a mile east of us, also had a horse and wagon. He would bring his horse over to our place one week and he and Charlie would go to town for the day. The next week Charlie would take our horse to Uncle Will's to make up a team and they would make the trip from there. I stayed home. The men didn't consider it necessary for me to go with them.

It turned out to be a poor year to start married life on a farm at Blue Mountain. Charlie had bought our cows on time and had plowed a field and planted it for hay. It had rained for two weeks before we were married but not one drop for three months that summer. That meant no hay.

By the time we bought hay, grain and our groceries, the cream check was used up. When spring came and no payment had been made on the cows all winter, the owner came after them. He even took the calves that had been born on our place. We did scrape up enough money to

Emily at 19

buy one of the cows. But one cow didn't provide enough cream to bring in any money to speak of.

One Sunday we went after blackberries and I walked right into a nest of bees. One stung me on a varicose vein and the darn leg wouldn't heal up. I would bleed at times so after about a week Charlie called a Dr. Hyde to come and see about it. After he reamed out the vein and sewed it up, the doctor said I was not supposed to be on it for a few days.

Somebody had to do the cooking and take care of me, and Charlie was no nurse. We called Earline who was still working for Herricks on the Elwha and Francis brought her out. That evening she acted nervous. We shared the same bed. She couldn't sleep but she wouldn't say why or what.

The next morning we found out why. There was a knock on the door and it was James Jacobs who lived with his folks on a ranch on O'Brien Road, just west of Blue Mountain.

Charlie said, "Hello, Jim. Come on in."

Jim said, "I came after my property."

"What property?" asked Charlie.

Jim pointed to Earline and answered, "That's it—right there. She's my wife."

We all knew Jim. He belonged to the young bunch who went to the Blue Mountain dances. While Earline was working at Elwha, Jim was forest ranger there and they fell in love and eloped to Seattle where they were married the week before Earline came to care for me. They hadn't told anyone. After they came back from Seattle, Earline took off her wedding ring and went back to work and Jim went to stay with his folks. The bridegroom had had enough of that kind of married life.

Earline had always been popular with the boys but nothing like she was at the time of her marriage to Jim. It turned out that when she decided to marry Jim she was also engaged to two other men. Between that and the fact she would have to face Mama it is no wonder she didn't tell anyone about being married.

One Sunday after my leg was getting better Charlie and I went to McDonnell Creek. I rode the horse. We got a nice mess of fish and we put them in a sack and hung it on the saddle. It was a warm day so when we got home Charlie cleaned the trout and put them in a strong salt solution to firm them up. They had softened in the heat. I fried them just like they were and I was proud of the way they cooked—but *salty* isn't the word!

Charlie said a few choice words but ate as many as he could. That night I woke up and could hear a clanking sound. Charlie had the water pail beside the bed and it was the dipper I heard clanking every time he took a drink.

Goldie Peterson was logging down near Dungeness (called Pumpkin Center in those days) so Charlie and my cousin Nat Broughton went to work for him in the spring of 1915. They walked the nine miles to work every Sunday afternoon and hiked home the next Saturday night after working all day.

Charlie quit working at the logging camp after about three months and remortgaged our forty acres. He had heard a team of colts was for sale by Bill Mayberrie who lived sixty miles west at Forks and Charlie needed the mortgage money to buy them. He was gone three days and each day was a new experience for him.

Charlie rode our horse out past Elwha and Lake Sutherland to Lake Crescent. There was no road around Lake Crescent but at East Beach a person and his horses could get on a barge and go nine miles to Fairholm at the lake's west end. There was a road from there.

The road was narrow, cut through timber that rose as high as twenty-story buildings on each side. It would get dark on the road but unless the sky was totally black Charlie could make his way by looking up and following the faint streak of light made in the sky where the timber had been cut out to make the road.

The horses were three years old and untrained. It was a

A big job for a "misery whip" saw

job just to catch them and put halters on and try to lead them. On the way back to Lake Crescent the colts jumped around and Charlie got a finger broken. When Charlie and some other men tried to get those horses on the barge to cross the lake—it was more of the same story.

No horse likes to walk on strange footing and there was nothing stranger to them than the deck of a barge. These colts weren't used to being loaded on anything and being forced to get on something that was always moving like the barge on the water scared them into a panic. Charlie finally had to blindfold the horses to get them loaded.

By the time they got to our home at Blue Mountain, Charlie and the horses were all in. The horses turned out to be a fine team though, and we had them five years.

Well, you might know, by now I was pregnant. I worked canning vegetables from our nice garden, milking the cow, and the doctor had told me to walk two miles every day so I was busy. We had been married four months.

When it came close to the time for the baby to be born, Charlie was working about fifteen miles away in Sequim, using the team to haul gravel for building roads. He boarded with his brother Elda and family so he didn't get home often.

Because Charlie couldn't be home, Mama came out from town where she had been living after coming back from Seattle. But I still milked the cow right up till the baby came, although my new shape made it quite a reach to the cow's teats.

Man on a spar tree. Two steam logging ''donkeys'' provide power below.

Road to Forks from Lake Crescent

Coming off the Lake Crescent ferry

Mama had suggested a spare room be fixed up to have the baby in and it was ready.

When the pains started the morning of June 27, 1915, Mama phoned Dr, Hyde. He said for me to walk. The walking was because of some internal problems the doctor thought might cause complications. Mama was to call the doctor again if the pains got worse. In the afternoon they got worse so Mama called. His car had a time getting up those Blue Mountain Road hills but Dr. Hyde arrived about five o'clock with his nurse "Aunt" Carrie Laurence.

Nothing much happened before meal time, about six, so the doctor and Aunt Carrie sat down with Mama and Charlie for dinner. It was Sunday, Charlie's day off. Everybody, except me, made themselves comfortable after dinner and spent the evening in conversation.

At 11:50 our first little girl was born, just ten minutes short of the end of the day of our first anniversary. Charlie named her Emily Genavive Lewis.

Aunt Carrie stayed for two weeks and Mama was there for six weeks after Emily came, but Mama didn't milk and although Aunt Carrie tried she got nervous, so did the cow, and the result was very little milk. After two weeks of that I was back doing the milking again.

We heated the house with wood in a pot-belly iron stove and Aunt Carrie didn't keep it hot enough so little Emily got three-month colic and I spent nights rocking the baby by pushing her buggy over a book on the floor to lull her to sleep.

Emily didn't seem to be getting enough nourishment either. When my milk was checked Charlie said, "What kid could get along with that oyster water?" It helped a lot when Emily got richer milk.

Grandmother Jennie with little Emily

Chapter 15

Dad Lewis had mortgaged the land before he deeded the forty-acre farm to Charlie. To get our team of horses, Charlie gave a second mortgage on the forty acres to Bill Mayberrie. Times were hard. We had one baby and within a year of Emily's arrival there was another baby on the way. We lost the forty acres through the mortgages.

Charlie had heard of the Macleay Estate consisting of hundreds of acres and located where R Corner is today, at the foot of Blue Mountain Road, and extending to the east toward Sequim.

He went to the Macleay Estate office in Sequim and signed a contract for forty acres of land at forty dollars an acre—a big price at that time—with a promise of an

R Corner home in its beginning

irrigation system that would bring water from the Dungeness River to the land. Although it is within ninety miles of land that receives up to two hundred inches of precipitation a year, the fifteen to twenty inches that falls on the area from R Corner to Sequim makes it almost impossible to raise garden crops without irrigation.

We needed a house to make the land a home so Charlie cut cedar logs from the Lewis homestead, although it had been repossessed. He hauled them to a small mill owned by Bill Boyd on Mount Pleasant Road. The logs were cut into rough lumber for our new home.

When the house was up it was fourteen feet by twenty feet, about the size of a fairly big living room. The outside walls were made of vertical planks with strips of wood called battens nailed over the cracks between the planks. There was no inside covering for the walls. Eventually we papered the kitchen part with old Saturday Evening Post magazines.

Charlie was a good carpenter and this fourteen by twenty building was supposed to become his shop and woodshed later. But sixty-four years went by and I'm still living in it. As I always say, every time we had an extra fifty cents we added on to the original building until it tripled in size, but that first house is still part of it.

Charlie and I and baby Emily moved down the Blue Mountain foothill to our new home May 1, 1916. Before we moved, there was a farewell party for us. My brother Francis gave us a lamp with a white shade on it. It had a round wick. When it was lit you could see all four corners of the room. It took so much more coal oil than most kerosene lamps we only used it when company came. But it was fun just to know we had such a lamp to look at.

Well, I thought we pioneered when we were kids—and now we were doing it again. There was land to clear, a well to dig, and a barn to build for the horses and the cow. For water, before the well was finished, we took the horses and wagon and two large rain barrels and drove a mile and a half to Seibert's Creek.

There were few dirt fills or high bridges to level out roads in those days, only low bridges which washed out sometimes in winter floods. It was rough going up one hill and down another.

To water the horses and cow we drove them down a steep trail to the creek where it passed near the house. The trail was too steep to bring barrels of water up.

Charlie made me a nice cooler that opened up from inside the one-room house. The cooler was on the north side of the house, away from the sun.

A back porch ran the full length of the west side of the house. There was a pail for washing and drinking water on the porch. Just inside the door from the porch was a small hole in the floor, and Emily, who was now eleven months old, packed and stuffed everything she could find into that hole. Charlie was in no hurry to fix it. Then one morning he couldn't find his suspenders. After considerable looking he discovered them in the hole. It didn't take him long to find a piece of lumber to close up Emily's hiding place.

When a person came through the door from the porch he passed the length of a rectangular table and its chairs on his left. On the west side of the room were two wood-burning stoves. They both gave off heat but one was for cooking. The heater was a pot-belly stove. (A single-sided wall doesn't do much to keep out the cold.) A chair was between the stoves, and a bed for Charlie and me and one for baby Emily were against the south wall.

A "sanitary cot" was to the left as you entered a door on the east side of the house. It was a mechanical trap. Its two sides folded up to make a one-person bed into a full sized one, but if only one side was pulled up and a person should get too far to that side, the whole bed tipped over. There were no legs under the sides.

Charlie once put up one side and stretched out. The bed went over and Charlie ended up partly on the floor with his elbow in a bucket of water left alongside. Mama slept on the bed when she visited us but managed to do it without any accidents, maybe because she was so small.

The small room was so crowded I got my hips bruised just walking between the furniture. But nothing really bothered us, unless it was the mosquitoes and fleas.

There were so many mosquitoes that little Emily looked like she had the measles all the time, from the bites. There were no ponds or swamps around the house where the insects could breed. We finally figured they must come from the moss on the ground. When it was dry, Charlie got a permit to burn the ground cover. That did the trick. The mosquitoes were gone.

Fleas were everywhere, even in the beds. Somewhere we heard that rock salt would kill them but when I put it between the sheets at the foot of the bed all I got rid of was Charlie. I forgot to tell him the pieces of salt were there and when he put his foot down in the sheets and they touched the salt he jumped out of the bed like a screaming Apache. We put the rock salt all over, even under the house, but it didn't work.

Lime turned out to be the answer. When we put it under the house the fleas disappeared.

Around the first of June in 1916—just about a month after we had moved in—a surveyor, whose name was Middlebrook, was hired by the Macleay Estate to survey its land. Mr. Middlebrook and his three helpers wanted to board with us. They had their own tents to sleep in so Charlie said, "Sure."

We got eleven-year-old Elston Isbell from Elwha to help me. He packed water, washed dishes, cut wood, and did other chores. The crew stayed six weeks. Even with Elston it sure was hard for me—I was very pregnant—but

Daughter Emily in front of surveyor-boarder's tent, 1916.

it helped with the bills.

Charlie had piled up a big bill for feed for the horses and cow. With the board money we paid the feed and grocery bills both. All I wanted out of it was money for two new shirts for the baby that was due soon, but I didn't get them. When the bills were paid there was no money left.

One day in late August, Charlie walked the four miles to our former home to see about the garden we had planted and he stayed all night. The next morning I knew the baby wasn't going to wait until September 17 as it was suppose to so I told Elston, who had stayed on with us, to walk up to the Emory house where there was a telephone and call Charlie, (We still had a phone at the homestead.) and tell him I needed him and for him to come right home.

But Elston didn't like to say I was sick so he just said, "Emily wants you to come home."

Well, we had been waiting for a fire permit so Charlie just supposed it had come so he took his time about coming home. When he did get there and saw what was going on he ran over to the Woodings', about three fourths of a mile, to phone the nurse who was with me when Emily was born, and also a doctor.

Nobody was home at Woodings' house and the doors were locked so Charlie came back home, and then walked two and a half miles to Willis Chamber's home. (For some reason Emory's phone wasn't available.)

When he phoned the doctor, he was out of town but the nurse Aunt Carrie was home so Charlie got our friend Harold Littlefield, who was a taxi driver, to go and get Aunt Carrie and bring her out to our place.

But by the time they arrived our daughter Helen was already there! For thirty years we argued. Dad, as I had begun calling him, claimed it was harder on his legs, running around trying to get help, than it was on me to have a baby by myself.

A well had been dug. It was an open hole in the ground with a winch supported over it. Turning a handle pulled a bucket of water to the surface.

We found out the winch could even be used to pull a man to the top of the well. While Charlie was digging for water he ran into a boulder that was too big for him to take out with a shovel. He planted a charge of dynamite under the rock, lit the fuse, and then hung onto the rope while I tried to pull him out by turning the winch.

I have never been very big, and cranking Charlie out of the well was almost more than I could handle. Charlie came close to being blasted out with the boulder.

For our first Christmas in our new home we had another improvement—a much-needed outhouse was built. Before, our toilet was all out and no house—just a log in the brush.

In June of 1918 Dad went to work as a carpenter for the Crescent Boxboard Mill on the Port Angeles waterfront so we moved to town where we lived rent-free in the three-bedroom "barn house" Alfred built. It was quite a change. Friends came to stay and Alfred spent Saturday nights and Sundays with us. We sold the horses and bought a second-hand Reo car.

Mama lived in town and occasionally we would get together and visit her friends. Helen, who was two years old, was with us when we went to a nice home to see a woman whose husband had just built the house. The bathroom was indoors and included a flush toilet, a very new thing at that time.

Not long after we got to the house Helen had to use the toilet. Toilets were put upstairs so there would be no odor in or near the dining room, so I took Helen upstairs.

Well, getting her on that toilet's white seat was bad enough, but when I flushed it—all hell broke out. Mama came to the bottom of the stairs and called to find out what was the matter with Helen.

After I got Helen calmed down we went downstairs again and continued our visiting. Now, the lady we came to see had plants in pretty flower pots in her front room. Some of the pots were empty and sitting on the floor. Mama, the lady, and I had been talking for quite a while when we heard a tinkling sound. Helen had pulled down her panties and was using one of the flower pots.

That stopped our visit. The lady of the house said, "Come back again" to Mama. But she just looked at me and said, "Goodby!"

In 1919 Dad was still working, but had been having some appendicitis attacks. He was pretty sick but he wanted to be home instead of in the hospital for the birth of our third child who was on the way. Dad was covered for medical care under the carpenters' union and May 21 was the deadline for receiving benefits. That was the day he walked to McGillivray Hospital on Eighth and Peabody Streets to be admitted for the operation.

Wouldn't you know, that same day my darn labor pains began. Mama lived real close to us so she came over to help with the girls, Emily, who was four, and Helen, who would be three in August. They were both sick with whooping cough at the time.

We phoned the nurse, a Mrs. Cloukie, to help with delivering the baby and were told she wouldn't be home

Port Angeles General Hospital, Dr. Donald McGillivray in center

until midnight—but she arrived in plenty of time.

Dr. Donald McGillivray got to our house around six in the morning. He roamed around the house and drank coffee for a while and then announced it was about time for the baby to arrive. It sure was. In fact it was already born while he and the nurse were in the kitchen.

It was May 22, 1919, and our third little girl Barbara was born. At nine o'clock that morning Dr. McGillivray operated on Dad and told him he had a beautiful little girl waiting at home.

Dad had said to me before he left, "If you don't have a boy this time I'm not coming home"—and do you know, he darn near didn't! Infection set in after the operation and if Dad hadn't been so strong and healthy he never would have come home to us.

A PIONEER TOWN

Sequim's Opera House is the center for 1909 May Day celebrations

The Pioneer Barber Shop in Sequim before 1911

An early Sequim store features wood cook stoves

Chapter 16

We stayed in town for a while after Charlie's operation because he had to report to Dr. McGillivray once a week for three months to have his side burned out to get rid of the infection.

For those three months we charged our groceries in a store on Eighth Street owned by Lum Sue. He was wonderful to us; never said a word about paying our bill. When Dad got work he paid it. He also bought a team of horses.

In September 1919 Charlie and Van Coolidge, a friend, moved to the ranch and started logging with the team. I stayed in town for a short while longer.

We had left the house full of furniture and unoccupied for several months and when we got back the only thing missing was a wine-making barrel. We found out a neighbor had borrowed it.

The logging stopped in December so my brother Alfred came out and helped put two much-needed bedrooms on our house. Charlie was a good carpenter so with logging and carpenter work, when he could find it, we did the best we could.

In 1920 women were allowed to vote so I registered in

Charlie Lewis logging, 1917

The irrigation ditch

Juan de Fuca Precinct. Dad didn't want me to register. He said women would just cancel the men's vote. I didn't like that.

In those days a person had to declare what political party he or she favored. I asked which one Dad had registered for. When I was told it was the Republican Party I swore I would live and die a Democrat.

There was still talk about getting an irrigation ditch like we had been promised. Dad had plans for a truck garden, to raise vegetables for sale. But a fight was brewing and it would have to be fought before the farms could get water.

A Port Angeles lawyer was the organizer of the ditch company. He had bought many acres of "land under the ditch," a term we used to indicate land the irrigation water would run through. Assessments were charged owners of land under the ditch. If they weren't paid for three years the ditch company took the land. There was no money coming in from assessments on any land the company took, of course. If the company didn't resell the land in seven years so taxes could be paid on it, the county took the property.

The lawyer, who was president of the ditch company, would only sell his own land, if he possibly could. The land the company had taken back because assessments weren't paid on it just sat there with no money coming in to help support the ditch, and there was a danger of losing it to the county.

The ditch company sold land for ten dollars a cleared acre and seven dollars a wooded acre.

We would go to the ditch association meetings and the lawyer, who always carried his briefcase while he was talking, would stand in front of a person who had enough nerve to talk back to him or ask a question and bang the case on the bench beside the talker and try to make him look foolish.

With all the dissatisfaction and troubles the ditch association was just about to fold up, so when election of ditch officers came in November those who had farms under the ditch and didn't like what was going on had their own meetings from house to house and decided to vote in new officers instead of the lawyer and his son, who was secretary.

On election night we were doing fine. It looked like we would win. Then sixteen land renters under the ditch came in and voted. They favored the lawyer and his son.

We understood renters couldn't vote and said so but the lawyer got up on the stage of the hall and read down in the rules of the ditch company just so far, but he didn't finish it. The renters really couldn't vote unless special water problems existed, and the problems didn't. But the lawyer didn't read that far down.

That threw it! The lawyer couldn't pull that stunt again. The next election Charlie was elected secretary, George Benson was president, and Wayne Chapman was treasurer. But we were still in a mess and the lawyer was still browbeating us.

It was decided to go to the state capital for help. There was no money for gas so some good Finn farmer neighbors came up with ten dollars and the new officers went to Olympia.

Down that old twisty Hood Canal Road we went, one hundred and twenty miles to the state capital. I can't remember the name of the man who was head of state irrigation projects, but he told us what he would do if it were him, and it was what we needed to hear.

Then he backed up what he told us.

One day after our trip the ditch officers were holding their monthly meeting and the lawyer was talking and banging his briefcase around, and the hall door opened. A man walked in and stood by the stove, listening.

The lawyer was telling us what we could and could not do. The man who had come in was the state official we had talked to in Olympia. He stepped up and introduced himself as the State Irrigation Director.

After he was through reading the irrigation laws and talking to the people at the meeting, we never again saw or had any trouble with the lawyer or his son.

Following this episode the community took a vote and removed the lawyer's name off the ditch and renamed it the Agnew Ditch, for Charles Agnew who came to the area in 1870 and made his home along what a few years later would become the Old Burlingame Road. Then it developed into the Port Angeles-Sequim Highway before Highway 101 was completed. About 1975 my nephew Don Jacobs bought the Agnew place and remodeled it.

Dad plowed a field and planted alfalfa, and in 1924 we bought forty-five fruit trees because by then the irrigation ditch was a sure thing. We planned a truck garden the next spring.

The need for me to be able to haul fruit and supplies in the old Reo meant I had to learn how to drive. Up to then I had never even thought of driving. Dad taught me to back in a road to get wood he had cut for sale. The road was crooked and narrow and by spring I knew how to drive.

The irrigation water came in 1925 and we made out pretty good on the truck garden. Then for two years, until weevils got into them, we had beautiful strawberries. The rows of the squat little plants with big red fruit hanging from them, stretching across the acre, were a great sight.

One day we were loading the car with flats of strawberries. Dad said, ''Go get me a board to put on the back seat.'' So I went into the woodshed. Looking for a board, I caught my foot on a loose strap and broke my ankle.

Poor Dad was disgusted with me, but I still cooked the meals for us and the berry pickers and kept tally on the pickers as they brought in the flats of berries.

Our girls were young but they helped too, and Dad paid them for picking. With some of the money they earned the girls went to town with their dad and bought me six glass goblets. I was so pleased, and I still have all six of them.

With the irrigation ditch battle over, I needed to be active in some other organization so I joined Fairview Grange in February 1925. It is a very worthwhile organization—more like a big family in each individual Grange.

Granges were responsible for today's rural mail routes, and our choice to vote as a Democrat or a Republican by the blanket primary, also things like working so hard for our Public Utility Districts.

Electricity was all around us, but we had to buy an

Daughters Emily, Helen and Barbara in dresses of the times

electric washing machine and sign to pay a lot of money just to get power from Puget Sound Power and Light Company for lights. Dad refused to buy the washing machine. He couldn't afford it anyway. So we had no electricity until about 1935.

While I was active in the Grange, I was elected to the positions of Lady Assistant Steward, Home Economics Chairman, Ceres, Flora, Pomona (twice), Secretary (for eighteen years), and the last position was Lecturer which I enjoyed the most. I also went to Aberdeen in 1936 as a state Grange representative. I really don't know how many times I was head of the Fairview Grange booth at the Clallam County Fairs. I sure enjoyed working on the booth. The Grange opportunities and the Grangers meant very much to me.

The Grange also made me develop my individuality. When the style came in where women could wear their hair short I wanted mine cut. But Dad said, ''No!'' His idea was that it would take away a woman's prestige, but most of all it would make her look more ''sexy and loose,'' as he explained it to me. He said a woman should keep that look just for her husband.

As time went on more and more women had their hair cut and I got a little braver. One day I said to Dad, ''It only costs a dollar for a haircut now.'' No answer. I wore my hair in a long braid and wanted it cut and, of course, I felt sorry for myself.

We had cattle in our pasture and one day I heard Dad out there yelling. I went out to see what was wrong and he hollered, "The cows broke out. Come help me get them back in!"

Outside the pasture fence were trees, stumps, and logs. I was jumping and running, trying to get the darn cows back into the pasture. I got up on a big log, trying to get ahead of the cows but I couldn't.

I sat down on the log to slide off. When I slid, my long hair caught in a knot sticking out from the bark. No Apache Indian ever yelled louder than I did.

Dad came running to see what I was hollering about and he got my braid loose. Then we got the cows back into their pasture and fixed the fence.

That night in bed before we went to sleep Dad said, "Next time we go to town you better get your hair cut, as long as it only costs one dollar."

When I had been a Granger for fifty years the Fairview Grangers sponsored a celebration. The work put into it was just beautiful. My nephew Dal Jacobs wrote a tribute to me and it was read by Eleanor Dilling. My daughter Bobbie and her husband Don sent a telegram from Alaska.

My nephew escorted me to my chair. Dal is over six feet tall and took long steps. I haven't walked that fast since I quit running after my girls when they were small, or at least not since chasing those cows.

A logging crew with horses

Chapter 17

Our three girls went to Macleay School, a few miles east, toward Sequim from home. No school buses came to our door in those days. The girls walked a mile to Burlingame Road (Old Olympic Highway) to catch the bus. And they had to be there by 7:30 in the morning. It was dark at that time two months of the school year.

When the girls did get to the school bus it was no luxury. Windows were broken and there was no heater. The seats were nothing but boards. The bus was built like a box. It was so noisy I could hear it start from where they kept it in an old no-longer-used school house about a mile away.

At Macleay School, Neva Cays Wheeler was one of their favorite teachers.

The girls were growing up, and with three of them in one bedroom there were times you didn't need a hearing aid to know what was going on in there.

Emily was always reading or making patterns from clothes she had seen in store windows downtown, a talent she has retained all her life. She never wanted to go outdoors with Helen and Bobbie. One day I insisted Emily go outside with the other girls and she fell on a box that had nails sticking up on it and cut her knee real bad. I took her into town to Dr. Donald Black who sewed the cut closed. We sometimes think we know what is best for our kids, but do we?

Every winter Helen would be home from school with a sore throat. I said, "It's her tonsils again, she needs them out," and Dad would say, "If she didn't need tonsils, God wouldn't have put them in there."

But one winter—I think Helen was thirteen—nothing we did helped her throat. There were cases of diptheria in Sequim so we called Dr. W. M. Davidson to come out from Port Angeles. When he came into the house, he said, "I smell diptheria." He later said, "If you hadn't called me she would have choked to death." The doctor gave her shots and swabbed her throat for phlegm. To keep down the danger of contagion we had to bury the phlegm and the health authorities sent some men to fumigate the house.

Helen came out of it but she was very weak for a long

Daughters Emily, 8, Helen, 7, Barbara, 4

time, and her troubles were not over.

We had a small kerosene-heated incubator to hatch baby chicks, but after they were hatched we had to put some chicks in a box with a jug of water to keep them warm through the night. One night when I fixed the jug the water was too hot and broke it so I threw it out. Later, in the yard, Helen helped me separate the big chicks from the small ones to keep the larger ones from getting all the food. (She was always cleaning and putting things in their proper place.) While Helen was stepping around the pen she ran her right foot into the broken glass jug and cut all the foot's ligaments.

I carried her part way to the house, then got the wheelbarrow to push her in.

George King, a neighbor, was on his way to town in his flat-bed Ford truck. I ran out in the road and got him to come in. He filled the cut full of flour to stop the bleeding and we put the old sanitary cot from the house onto the

Early school bus

back of his truck. We laid Helen on it and I sat on the cot alongside her all the way to Port Angeles to Dr. Davidson's hospital.

The doctor said flour was one of the best things to put on the cut and he had no trouble cleaning the wound and tying the ligaments together.

The poor girl was in bed most of the summer but she got back use of her foot.

Bobbie, who was three years younger than Helen and four years younger than Emily, never could stand to see anybody or any animal hurt. Any bird that died was buried and a stick put in the ground to mark the place.

One day Dad killed a mouse that had a nest with baby mice whose eyes were closed yet. Bobbie took the little mice and we found her behind the kitchen stove feeding them milk with an eyedropper.

Bobbie prepared a lunch for us one day while we were stringing wire. Dad worked hard digging holes and putting in fence posts. When he was ready to string the barbwire on them he put an iron rod through the roll of wire and I took one side and he took the other. It was hard work.

Bobbie's lunch was in one of her many make-believe playhouses she made out of stovewood, and she wanted us to come and eat with her. Dad wasn't too set on it but we went. I think Bobbie took a leaf off of everything growing and put sour cream and salt on it. If I use my imagination a little I think I can still taste it.

All three girls stuck together. I remember one time Emily did something that provoked her dad and he slapped her and told her to go to their bedroom.

Right away Bobbie took up for Emily so Dad said, "You go to our bedroom!"

Then Helen went to her dad, "You're an old skunk, and there's only two bedrooms. Where are you going to send me?" Dad had to laugh by this time. Dad was very proud of his three girls and loved them very much.

The summer Helen had diptheria Dad logged for a Mr. Shore who had a mill situated by Wooding Road, now called Shore Road. Dad had five hundred dollars coming for logs he sold to the mill when one night the mill burned. Laborers at the mill had to be paid, according to law, but not the loggers, and Dad had no written agreement with Shore. So we were out the five hundred dollars which was quite a blow to us. We needed the money to pay our feed bill and buy clothes and food.

Emily was now ready for high school. She wanted to be a teacher. At that time Sequim High School was not accredited so she went to Port Angeles High School. Emily stayed in town with my mother two school years. When Helen started to high school two years later she worked for her board and room in several homes in Port Angeles.

One year we had an old Chevrolet for them to commute with. Emily never learned to operate a car so Helen did all the driving. The Chevy had windshield wipers but you had to crank them by hand from inside the car. Helen was too short to reach the handle so Emily operated the swipes. The girls picked up LaVerne Almaden and Alice Brager who also went to high school in Port Angeles. That helped pay for the gas.

In 1929 I was operated on for what you use to refer to as "female troubles." The operation was successful. I felt stronger and better than I had for years. Dad had to sell two heifers to pay the hospital bill. We never were able to pay Dr. J. C. Hay for the operation, but he never sent us a bill anyway.

The year 1930 came and everybody was having a tough time, including us. But Dad teaching me how to drive a car paid off. A friend of ours was manager of the Grange Store in Carlsborg, between our home and Sequim, and he needed a clerk. One woman had applied but she couldn't drive, so our friend said, "You are a good driver, Emily, so come try it." The only way to get there was to drive.

I couldn't even make change—never had that much to practice on. John Ward brought his wife to Carlsborg every morning—she was postmistress there—then he came over to the store and taught me how to make change.

I received fifty dollars a month, but the agreement was I would spend twenty dollars of that for groceries at the store. That left thirty dollars to take home, and there was still more groceries and cow feed to buy.

I'll say right here, I worked at the store three years and I never came home one single night that the girls didn't have a nice dinner cooked and Bobbie had the woodbox filled. In the summertime Bobbie and Helen worked in the pea fields to buy their school clothes.

Now the girls were teenagers they were old enough to go out and there were real nice dances at Fairview Hall just down the road. I thought the girls were too young to go alone so I took them. The rules were that there was no leaving the hall until after the dance, and that they came home with me.

Dad didn't like me going to the dances so I was glad when a friend of ours Lawrence Brager—who was about ten years older than our girls—came on Saturday nights and took them to Fairview and brought them home.

The girls were becoming ladies.

Carlsborg

Chapter 18

The Grange Store burned in 1932—gas pumps, kegs of nails, barrels of oil, meat department, sacks of feed—everything. It was a terrible loss to the stockholders.

It was a shock to me. I didn't know anything about it until I drove into Carlsborg to go to work the morning after the fire. I always get cold easy and I hate to be cold, so I had a habit of trying to catch a glimpse of the store from a place where it could be seen between buildings as I got close to it—to see if there was smoke coming from the chimney.

Rudy Luthi, who ran the store, was scared to death of fire so he sometimes didn't have the stove going before I got there. If I couldn't spot smoke coming out of the chimney it would be a cold morning at the store.

I was late to work the morning after the fire so I didn't bother taking a peek to check for smoke. The full impact hit me when I rounded the corner just up the street from the two-story building. It was gone. The Grange Hall was in the second story. The records were burned and even the piano destroyed.

It was in the Grange Hall the fire started. There had been a dinner there that evening and the Grange had decided to start using paper plates. The plates were put in the stove to burn just before everyone left. The fire got too hot and started the building burning.

The big Carlsborg Mill Company owned a store building in Carlsborg but were not using it so the Grange and stockholders rented it. It was smaller than the other building, and, of course, less room meant less trade but it was the best place available.

In the fall of 1933 one of the stockholders' daughters needed work so there went my job. I was home until April of 1934 and then I got another job—but not in a way I thought was fair.

Dad had borrowed money on his life insurance to buy a truck but the Great Depression was getting worse and he lost the truck and the life insurance. And we owed a four hundred and thirteen dollar grocery bill.

I remember that real well, because of what Dad did to me. The bill was at the Help Yourself Store in Port Angeles on the west side of Lincoln Street between First and Second Streets. As far as I know it was the first serve-yourself grocery in town. It was owned and operated by Mr. and Mrs. William G. Manspeaker—lovely people. Mr. Manspeaker died and his son came from California to join Mrs. Manspeaker in the store.

One day the son came out to see Dad and two days later he came out again. The men did the talking but just before the son left he came over to me and said, "I'll see you Monday morning at eight o'clock."

After he left I asked Dad what he meant and Dad said, "Oh, you're going to work that grocery bill out." Of course, I cried—Dad use to call me his crybaby. It took me two weeks after I started working before I could see I should have been glad to be able to help out. But I still think Dad could have asked me first!

The store had a wonderful stock of food. Oranges had to be piled a certain way each morning—and one lady use to take the bottom ones and they would all fall.

The son had big ideas for a small-town store and that was the end of it. Poor Mrs. Manspeaker. I felt sorry for her. People said she stayed in her bedroom and wouldn't even come out to eat.

I got fifteen dollars a month to take home and the rest of my wages went on the bill. I got only one full check before the store closed.

Charlie found work and had to use our car so the last two weeks I worked I got out on the road real early and was lucky getting rides. Twice a state patrolman picked me up and took me to the store. I had worked there a year and learned a lot more about how to be a good clerk, something that was going to come in handy.

When Emily graduated from high school in Port Angeles we were pretty short of money. All Dad had was his blue wedding suit. My sister Earline fixed my old coat so I went.

Then Emily was married June 1, 1934. I was still working so we were able to get Dad a much deserved new suit and we had a nice wedding for her and her husband Orel Goodman at the Fairview Grange Hall.

It was also in 1934 we finally became owners of our land, but not without a problem. When a survey was

R Corner Store, 1945

made in 1916 it was discovered the amount of land we thought we had was not the same as the survey showed, so we bought twenty more acres. Then the land salesman we bought from ran off and no record of payments could be found. Barbara Macleay, owner of the land, asked Charlie how much land he wanted. He took thirty acres, paid up.

February 1, 1936, my oldest brother Alfred who was running a logging camp for the Eli Woolworth Company on the Soleduck River was hurt very badly. It's called in logger talk "getting hit with the bite of the line." The line was a big cable attached to a spar tree. It had "hooks" on one end that were used to pick up and load logs on a logging train.

June 1 they sent Alfred to Providence Hospital in Seattle. He had an operation on his head and back, but Alfred passed away July 7. No man ever worked harder to make a go of everything he undertook than my brother did.

Our second girl, Helen, married Chad Brown June 13, 1936.

When the state put in Highway 101 it took thirty of our forty-five fruit trees and our alfalfa field—putting quite a dent in our farming—so Dad came up with the idea to build a store east of the house. We needed money, of course, so Dad told me to go to the First National Bank in Port Angeles to see if we could get a mortgage on our thirty acres. I never did know why he sent me instead of going himself.

By golly, I was never so belittled in all my life, the way that banker talked to me. You might know—I cried. Then Dad said to go to the First Federal Savings and Loan Association. Do you know—they sent a man out that afternoon and we got the mortgage.

Dad worked hard on making the store look attractive. He put in the rock buildings at Sequim Bay State Park to get the money for building the store. He was so impressed by the rocks that he used them for the storefront. Today, the rock, and the two pillars made from tree trunks, are almost as sound as ever.

We opened our store on July 27, 1937. Business was slow at first and we had to buy just half-cases of canned goods at a time, which cost us more per can than buying full cases, and we could only afford to get two or three loaves of bread a day from the delivery man.

But we kept growing. Neighbors were neighbors in those days; even if the goods cost them a little more, they traded with us.

We wanted to sell wine but we had to apply for a license first. When we went to Port Angeles to get it, they had to have the name of the store and we didn't have one. I said to Dad, "It's always been *your* ranch, *your* girls, *your* horses. I wish just for once something could be *ours!*" So Dad said, "Let's call it R Corner." And it's still called by that name.

When we opened our store the state was using aluminum tokens and pennies for paying sales tax. The tax was two cents on the dollar and the tokens—between the sizes of a nickel and a quarter and with a hole in them—were used to pay tax on amounts between even dollars.

If the purchase came to one dollar and twenty cents you added two cents for the dollar and one token for the twenty cents. The bill would come to one dollar and twenty-two cents and one token—which was a headache to keep track of. The tokens were each worth one-fifth of a cent in tax.

In 1938 our oldest daughter Emily and her husband Orel had a baby born June 17—our first grandchild—and a *boy!* He was named Terrence Garth Goodman. On July 7, 1938, our second grandchild was born to Helen and Chad. They had a baby girl. She was named Marcia Lorraine Brown.

In 1939 we moved into living space Dad had built onto the rear of the store. It had complete plumbing—the first time in our lives we had had a bathtub.

Emily and family lived near us and Helen and Chad lived in Port Angeles. It was so nice to have the kids so close to us. They came home often, bought their groceries from us, and always came to our house for holidays. Terry got to be quite a Grandma and Granddad's boy.

In the summer of 1939 Barbara, our youngest girl, left for Cordova, Alaska, with her friend Esther Gerber to work in a clam cannery, after taking one year of business college. When Bobbie was getting clothes ready to go she made herself a pretty, long dress. I said, "All you will do is wear old blue jeans up there."

"Oh," Bobbie said, "I'm going to meet my Prince Charming on the ship going up," and I'll be darned if she didn't meet Don Conover.

After canning season was over Don and a friend flew from Anchorage down to Cordova to get Bobbie. Bobbie wrote first and asked me what I thought about her going to Anchorage. She and Don had been corresponding while she was in Cordova. Bobbie said if I thought she should come home she would.

After reading her letter I thought it all out and I wrote to her and said, "You take time to ask yourself if you really think enough of this man to live with him the rest of your life, or would you rather look around some more?"

Well, Bobbie and Don were married February 1, 1941, and Bobbie is still Mrs. Don Conover. Alaska is a long way away and I have missed her very much.

By 1940 we had the mortgage paid off on the store and were buying a big open-top refrigerator. We told the appliance store owner not to put the contract in First National Bank where I had been insulted before, but he did. We never missed a payment and when the refrigerator was paid for the banker said, "We would like your trade; you are responsible people." After my experience with him we wouldn't change.

When World War II came along—that was awful! We had to go to the Ration Board for sugar, meat, coffee, butter and gasoline books, and more tokens were put to

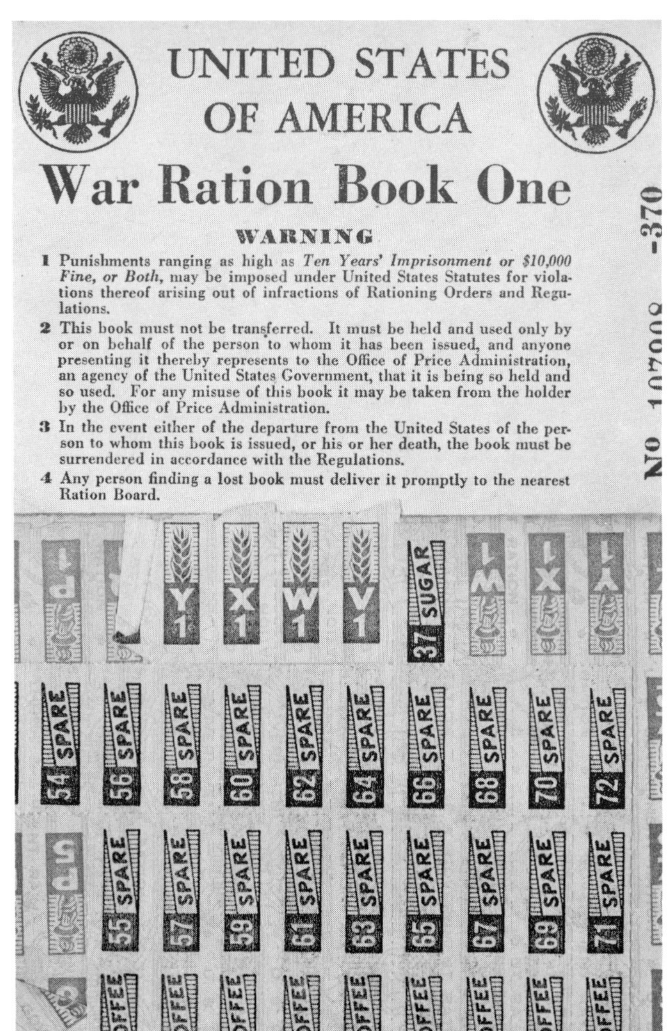

Ration stamps

use. The meat was red; sugar was white, I can't remember anymore what the blue token was for.

Stamps were used for rationing gasoline. One night about midnight somebody was hammering on our front door. Dad said, "To heck with them!" He wouldn't get up. The party kept banging so I got up to see what he wanted. It was gas for his motorcycle. The stamp he had was for a truck but at that time of night I gave him some gas and took the stamp.

I had all my teeth pulled at one time and the nicest thing about it was that I lost ten pounds. At that time you went without your dentures for three months after the teeth were out. That was embarassing when you worked all day in a store.

Edwin Champion, who was tighter with money than the bark is on a tree, came to the store one day and said, "Peg (I was often called by that name), I'll give you fifty cents if you can whistle a tune." I did, and I got my fifty cents too!

The payoff was when a customer came to the store and I asked him what he wanted. I coughed and we heard a noise, and there lay my lower teeth on the floor, right between his feet. One good thing, I didn't know him and I never saw him again.

Chapter 19

My half-brother Hubert Campbell, who was ten years old when he was left behind with an aunt in Illinois at the time the rest of our family moved west, suddenly came back into our life.

A couple years after my mother and father separated, Dad went to India to become a Buddhist priest where he stayed until Aunt Emma brought him home when he asked to come at the start of World War I. Hubert was only sixteen when my dad left, and had been living with him for a time in Seattle, learning to be a waiter.

Later my dad went to Texas where he died in 1925. I never saw him after he left the Blue Mountain homestead.

The restaurant people he worked for liked Hubert and made a home for him. When the couple sold their restaurant and moved to Edmonton, Canada, they took Hubert with them. He lived there thirty-five years, was married and he and his wife had two girls. Hubert's wife left him and he sold his home and he and his youngest daughter Irene came to Port Angeles.

His money was soon gone and Hubert needed a job so we asked him to come stay with us and help in the store. This he did, and he turned out to be a big help to us. He eventually left the store. He needed more money so he went to work at Angeles Creamery in town.

Dad began feeling bum. The doctor in Port Angeles thought he was having gall bladder trouble.

We heard of a man named Hughy, who, by rubbing you, could heal you. Our Helen, her husband Chad, and their daughter Marcia moved into our place and Helen and Hubert ran our store. Dad and I moved to Centralia in the southwest part of the state where this man Hughy lived. We stayed about two months while Dad took treatments.

Dad finally declared the man's name should be Hooey instead of Hughy and we went home.

Soon Dad became a very sick man but he fought doing anything about it. Helen, who could always do more with her dad than anyone else, insisted he go to Virginia Mason Hospital in Seattle so he did.

The doctors examined Dad and said he needed an operation. We came home and were back in Seattle again in a few days. Dad was operated on September 17, 1941—his birthday. We were there two weeks. It was cancer.

Before we left the hospital the doctor called me into a room and said, "Your husband is a very sick man, and we give him a year to live. But if he is as strong a man as I think he is it will be longer."

When I came out of the room to where Dad was he said, "What did that doctor show you? You're as white as a ghost."

Dad was as strong as the doctor thought.

In July 1941, after Dad became sick, Bobbie and her husband Don, who we had never seen, came down from Alaska. They lived with us about six weeks. Don found work and they moved to Port Angeles.

In 1942, after the United States got into World War II, Don enlisted in the Army and in 1943 he was in Idaho

Brother Hubert in 1940 and as teenager

training to be a glider pilot. Bobbie was living with Dad and me at the store.

Emily and Orel had had another baby (our third grandchild), a boy named Earl Scott Goodman, born December 2, 1942. They lived across the highway from us and one night Bobbie stayed with the boys while Emily and Orel went to a movie in town.

It was about eleven o'clock and Dad and I had just got in bed and Dad had said, "This is the life, when after a long day in the store you can rest until morning." The phone rang and it was Bobbie. She said, "I'm sick, my water broke. What am I to do?"

I turned to Dad and told him and he said a few choice words and then told me to tell Bobbie we would be right up to get her. Mrs. Sabra Winters lived right across the road from us. She came over to the house to stay with Emily's two boys, and we started to the hospital with Bobbie.

The government had restricted the use of headlights on cars. We had a Chevrolet and with the two small parking lights you were allowed to use to keep from being spotted in case of an air raid we could hardly see the highway. There was no choice but to go slow, and it was Bobbie's first baby—she just knew it was coming any minute.

I'll say right now it was quite a ride that night but we got there in plenty of time. It was morning before the baby was born. There was only one complication—the baby had to be turned before it was delivered. Bobbie and Don's son was born February 7, 1943, and was named Dale Lewis Conover. He was our fourth grandchild.

Don, who was still training to be a glider pilot, was sent to Texas and Bobbie and little Dale went with him. It was quite a change for Bobbie, after living in Port Angeles and Alaska.

They found a three-room house. Her washing machine was the bathtub. The air conditioning consisted of wetting the roof to get the house cool enough to sleep in. There were all kinds of bugs she had never seen and didn't want to see. But one day a sow bug was crawling across the floor. It was like the ones at home. She didn't kill that one. She picked it up and held it—like it was a piece of home itself.

In front of the better houses offered for rent were painted signs: NO DOGS OR YANKEES ALLOWED, Bobbie said. The only time Bobbie could buy sugar or butter was if she was lucky enough to be in the store when no Texan was there. The store clerk wouldn't be caught selling rationed items to a Yankee.

Don was sent to North Carolina and then overseas. Bobbie and Dale, along with a friend who was coming to Washington with her three-month-old baby, didn't waste any time getting home.

Bobbie lived at the store for quite a while, until Helen and her two children, Marcia and the new baby Gary, came to live in our house, then Bobbie moved in with Helen. All the girls lived near us now.

Helen's husband Chad was in the Navy and was soon to be shipped out. Before he left, Chad and Dad fixed up the house. They put in a bathroom, hot water plumbing—the first the house had had in its thirty years—and a brand new shake roof which has never leaked.

As I said, Don was overseas. His glider was sent out on an attack on the Germans. Airplanes were to follow to provide the troops protection after the gliders landed, Don said. There were many Germans near them so our boys crawled to a creek and lay there all night in the water. Our planes didn't come until morning.

Chad was shipped out June 1, 1944. He was a third class radarman. While he was on duty watching for Japanese air raids, Chad said that one day, first he heard, and then he saw, a fleet of Japanese airplanes coming right for the ship. He radioed instructions to change course and kept the fleet from getting hit.

Chad came home in December 1945. The cooks forgot to order enough salt for the trip back so the food was *blah* but nobody minded much. Nothing could dim the pleasure of coming home.

In 1945 our oldest daughter Emily and her husband Orel sold their place on Blue Mountain Road and moved down to the Burlingame Road, not far away, where they lived in the old Knutson house. Bobbie and Don and little Dale moved back to Anchorage. Helen and Chad and young Marcia and baby Gary moved into our old house across from the store. Dad and Chad built an addition onto the store, including a storage room.

On March 1, 1946, Chad and Helen bought the store and moved in. Dad was failing and could only work a little at a time. We moved back to our house and bought a bunkhouse from the Filion Mill in Port Angeles and Dad joined it to the house. He added a kitchen and a bathroom and built on a utility room.

The added space came in handy soon. My mother had lived alone since 1914. After Earline, Alfred and I were married, she worked for a year and then bought a little home at Fourteenth and Cedar Streets on Pine Hill in Port Angeles. Alfred and his wife lived just a block away so Mama was well taken care of.

Mama gave piano lessons to many children, and she had lots of good friends. She also loved to paint pictures, and she loved to go. If anyone came to see if she wanted to go with them Mama would stop right in the middle of washing clothes.

It was sure different than the way Charlie brought me up. I thought it was awful at the time, to just drop things and leave, but now I don't know. You either go when they ask you or you don't get to go at all.

Mama was now 87, very forgetful and she didn't eat half the time. My brother Francis, who was going to Petersburg, Alaska, to work in a sawmill, said, "I'll pay for moving her things out, Emily, if you will take care of Mama."

So in May of 1946 Mama moved into the apartment Dad had built onto our house. Mama ate with us.

You think you are doing what's best—but are you? Mama was so mixed up and unhappy in strange surroundings and without seeing her friends as often.

U.S. AT WAR

World War II battleships

Navy men drill during visit to Port Angeles in World War I era

Chapter 20

In August of 1946 Dad wanted to go to the Three Lakes area in the Olympics, a place not far from Hurricane Ridge where we had spent a vacation while living at Elwha. Dad loved to fish.

We had already spent a week camping near P. J. Lake (named for P. J. Williams, a Port Angeles jeweler) on Hurricane Ridge with our good friends Lloyd and Hilda Brown. But Dad wanted to get out into the woods and do as much fishing as he could and fishing was good at the lake.

We wanted to stay two weeks in the Three Lakes area and that meant a lot of food, bedding, and other supplies had to be packed in. We couldn't find anyone with horses so we hired Jim Summerville, who was a farmer neighbor, and his two boys to back-pack our gear to the lakes. My brother Francis and his wife Goldie went in

Hurricane Ridge

View from near Obstruction Point

with us and stayed the first week.

We drove to Hurricane Ridge up a zig-zagged switch-backed dirt road that climbed 5,000 feet up from the Elwha River in four miles through big, dense timber at first and then as we got higher the timber thinned out and got smaller until at the ridge there were large meadows and only patches of scrawny, weather-beaten trees. The eight miles along the ridge to Obstruction Point was not so steep.

After we left the cars at the Point we started walking Four Miles Trail. The first lake was Moose Lake, the second was Lake Etta and the last Gladys Lake. We were going to Etta. The trail went straight down. By the time we got to Moose Lake and stopped for a breather, my legs and Goldie's were so tired they couldn't have shook more if we had come face to face with a black bear.

Years ago these lakes were named by one of our homesteaders, Amos Cameron and his brother-in-law, a Mr. Moose. Since the government has taken our mountains into Olympic National Park the names have been changed around.

Well, we all hiked to Lake Etta. It was deeper than Moose Lake and had a small natural prairie on one side and mountains on the other, and a little creek of good water running through the prairie to the lake.

We put a heavy canvas over the stove Dad built out of rocks, to keep the rain off. We used the stove to cook on and it was our only supply of heat, to sit or stand by. Then we put up a tent for sleeping and a place to store our clothes and food.

Francis and Dad fished every day. Goldie and I talked, fished (without much luck), took long walks, and cooked—those men were always hungry.

We took an alarm clock with us. Dad said one night I had better set the alarm. I told him, "I don't know why. You have gotten up every morning at six o'clock since we've been married and that's thirty-two years now."

It rained some every day. We moved our tent four times to get out of water. Our beds were damp and cold so we made a "heater" by putting rocks in the fire and then, when we were ready to go to bed, we put them in a pail and set them in the tent. It helped.

One day the sun came out long enough to put our bedding out to air and to put fresh air in our mattress. That seemed to make the bed warmer.

Dad put a smooth log beside our stone fireplace. To keep warm we'd sit down and warm our backs and then turn and warm the front. Believe it or not we both wore a hole in the seat of our pants. Dad was awful thin so the hole in his pants was because of his bones. I was awful fat in those days so mine was from weight.

The National Park men had built a concrete biffy but there were no walls or roof. It just sat out on the prairie before God and everybody. Dad had said before we left home, "We won't have a lot of people around us up there." I kept track of the visitors and in two weeks forty-six people passed through, and, of course, used the biffy.

One morning I went up to it and somebody had left the lid up. I was about to stand up and leave when I felt something! It was a darn squirrel trying to get out.

I was yelling my head off! Dad came a running to see what it was all about. He was disgusted that I would get so excited by a little squirrel. I wonder how he would feel with a squirrel running up between his legs.

The weather was cold and nasty and I wanted to go home but Dad said, "Not until you catch some fish!" So I caught twenty-one fish, but they were small. I fished from the shore but Dad used a small boat that was built and carried in to the lake by Ansel Jackson and his nephew early that summer. Ansel had told Dad where he hid it and for us to use it but to be sure and hide it again before leaving—which Dad did. The Park officials don't allow boats on the high-country lakes.

I still am thankful Dad didn't make me get into that boat. I hate water!

The morning Jim Summerville and his boys were coming to pack us out I put on a big kettle of beans and I still have never seen three men get away with so many beans. They ate all four quarts.

When it got close to time to go home, Dad built a dam in the creek so it would form a pool. He caught about twenty big trout and kept them alive in the pool so they would be fresh to pack out for our friends.

When we were eating our last breakfast up there, Dad said, "Eat up all the left-overs." So I ate the prunes and I still say they were the sweetest prunes I ever ate. But when I got down to the last of them I spooned up the juice. It was pretty lumpy. The mice had apparently been in it the night before.

While we were there I said to Dad, "This is August 29th, Helen's birthday. I wonder who will make her a sour-cream birthday cake." She always teased me about my sour-cream birthday cakes.

Well, we got Jim and his boys packed and they started up Four Miles. Dad hid the boat and we started up the hill to Obstruction Point where our car was. Dad got pretty tired coming out but never a word of complaint.

The next month Dad and I and the Browns drove to Jackson Ranger Station, now called the Hoh Rain Forest Visitors Center and Campground—more good fishing and lots of elk around us. One night the elk started tramping around and around our tent. We sure didn't sleep, and we were darned scared too!

On Sunday, Hilda and I fried chicken and fixed potatoes and fresh corn on the cob. Just as we sat down to eat the Old Man up above us let loose. It rained only like it can do in the Hoh River Valley where it is not unusual to get twelve feet and more of rain a year. We grabbed everything and ran into our tent and ate dinner there.

On that same trip we drove down to Oil City near the mouth of the Hoh. It was no city, not even a town, but in the early 1900s some company sold building lots for houses there but nothing much came of it. Not far from there a company drilled an oil well that produced some high-grade oil but not much of it.

We drove on down to the mouth of the Hoh where we camped. We went home the next morning. I'm so glad Dad had those camping trips. He was in more pain now.

Three Lakes area

Chapter 21

In 1947 we received a letter from our Bobbie in Alaska. She was expecting another baby in June. She and her husband Don were having a hard time making a living and they wanted us to come up and take care of our grandson Dale while Bobbie was in the hospital having the baby.

Mama stayed with my cousin Marie Atterberry. Aunt Julia lived with Marie and her husband Ray so Mama and Aunt Julia had quite a time, according to Marie. Each one tried to take care of the other. Mama would put some item of food on her plate and Aunt Julia would take it off, saying Mama shouldn't have it; it wasn't good for her. Then Mama would put it back on.

Dad and I went to Seattle June 21 to fly to Alaska. Flight insurance was offered at the airport so we bought some. Dad made his out to me and I made mine out to Dad. That was good for a laugh later, when we realized that if the darn plane had gone down we would both have been killed so the insurance wouldn't have done either of us any good.

It was my first air trip and nobody in his right mind could be more scared than I was. Dad never scolded me, but I hung on to his knee and, believe it or not, after we got to Don and Bobbie's it took two pressings with a wet cloth and a hot iron to get the wrinkles out of his pants.

The airplanes were not pressurized in those days and my ears plugged up even though I chewed the gum the steward gave us. My legs and feet swelled and it was three days before I could get my shoes on.

A big piece of ice came off the wing and scraped along the plane. I yelled, "We are ripping open!" Poor Dad. He grabbed me and said, "It's nothing but some gawd damn ice sliding off."

Anyway, we got there and Bobbie was darn tickled to see us. Our grandson remembered us from when he lived near us down home.

Going to Alaska was quite an experience for Dad and me. It was our only trip in our thirty-three years of married life—except to go to Seattle when Dad was operated on.

Alaska at that time was just really starting to grow. It was like our homestead days. The people who moved up there at first were real people. They could take the hard times and still be generous and helpful to others.

Bobbie was cooking for the five of us on a two-burner hot plate. After two days of that, Dad came home with an electric stove with an oven.

Don had a brother Dean who lived next door to him. One day Don, Dean and some friends went to Ship Creek to fish and came home with quite a few. (Dad was too sick to go.) They cleaned the fish and hung them on the clothes line. When Dad got up the next morning I'm glad no one could hear him! "Never heard of such a thing. They'll be fly-blowed!" he ranted. Because of the long daylight hours he was sure the blow flies would have been around and laid eggs in the fish, but it was too cold for blow flies up there.

As soon as breakfast was over, Dad started looking for a big wooden box or some lumber to make a smokehouse out of. He finally found two big boxes and put them together and smoked the fish. There were lots of raspberries on the kids' place so between smoking fish and picking berries Dad was a busy man.

One evening after the fish were smoked, neighbors came over to Bobbie and Don's house with two cases of beer. They ate all the fish and drank all the beer.

It was only ten blocks to downtown Anchorage. We walked down right after we got there and on our way home we passed a yard where the owner had just planted baby cabbage plants. That was June 22. We came back to R Corner July 21, and those cabbages in that one month's time were all grown and ready to eat. I'll never forget it.

Lots of people were either building their homes or having them built. Dad, who was a darn good carpenter, would walk down to watch the men working on the buildings and he would come home just furious! He would say, "Those damn fools get big wages and don't know one end of the hammer from the other."

As time for the baby to be born came closer it wasn't hard to see Don wanted another boy. Then when Bobbie got him up around two o'clock in the morning to take her to the hospital, Don was so excited he kept saying, "What if it's a girl? What will we do?" Bobbie told him, "Well, I guess we will just keep it and give it a girl's name."

His worries were for nothing. The baby was a boy—Robert.

During the 1930s' depression days President Franklin D. Roosevelt opened up Matanuska Valley to homesteaders. After bobbie got home and was feeling well enough to ride, Dean Conover loaned his car to Don and we drove to Matanuska which was sixty miles from Anchorage.

By 1947 there were schools, churches, grocery and feed stores, a creamery experiment station and lots of liquor stores. To grow their cabbages, they put tar paper down on the ground and made a hole for each plant. I have never seen such big cabbages—two Irishmen couldn't shake hands across them. Flowers too, of all kinds. No real season for each kind. Everything comes up at the same time.

On our way back to Anchorage we stopped to eat a lunch at the Knik River. Later, Don and Bobbie's children called the big high bridge over the river Dad's Bridge because Don had worked on it before he was married.

We enjoyed ourselves in Anchorage. With all the building going on and Dad being a good carpenter I am pretty sure that with our Bobbie living there, we would have moved up, if we were younger and Dad had been well. But Dad was getting weaker, so when the month was up we flew back to Seattle. It was late at night when we landed.

We went to a hotel—no vacancy. We walked to another hotel. It also had no vacancy, except the bridal suite. The clerk told us we could have the room at the usual cost of other rooms in the hotel. It was one o'clock in the morning and we were tired so we said we would take it.

The room was on the top floor. When we walked into it there was still a lot of rice on the floor, and it had twin beds. I was glad the walls didn't have ears after listening to Dad for twenty minutes giving me his idea on twin beds in a bridal suite.

We arrived at R Corner July 21. Dad was much weaker, but he never complained. On Tuesday, September 2, I called good old Dr. Hay. He drove out that evening and he and Dad talked about fishing and had a beer. When Doc was leaving he said, "If Charlie isn't better in the morning bring him in."

On Wednesday, September 3, I took Dad to the hospital. I never left the hospital in Port Angeles for two weeks. The first week I sat in a chair and slept some. My cousin Geneva brought a folding camp-cot down, which sure helped.

Dad passed away September 17, 1947, on his sixty-second birthday.

Chapter 22

The girls came home, even Bobbie from Alaska with her three months old baby Robert. There is nothing so comforting at a time like this than having your children come home to be with you. Emily and Orel with their two boys Terry and Scott were there. Helen and Chad and their one girl Marcia and two boys Gary and Ron came.

Dad, who always wanted boys, would sure have enjoyed his six grandsons, and one granddaughter.

Before Dad passed away he said, ''I worry about you, Peg; you're so insecure.'' He was older in years, and lots more experienced in wordly ways than I was. If he were working away from home, before he left for work my day's chores were planned out for me. My mother was very strict that way too, so I guess I was used to it.

Dad was right. I was like a chicken who can't swim and is thrown out into deep water. I was just stripped for three months after Dad passed away. I could not cry or believe he was gone. I couldn't sleep and I would get up at two in the morning and play the piano or make bread. I just couldn't seem to get adjusted.

In November of 1947, two months after Dad passed away, my oldest daughter Emily Goodman, her husband and their two sons came to live with me. They had sold their store near Everett.

I guess I upset them with my actions—getting up nights and so forth—so one day Emily said, ''Mom, sit in a chair, smoke a cigarette, and don't get up until you're through.'' Well, I always had lit Charlie's cigarettes while

Lincoln Street, Port Angeles, in 1940s

Looking north down Laurel Street, Port Angeles, in 1940s

he was driving the car. I liked the taste but being a good wife I had never smoked a cigarette. Dad would have had a fit if I had taken up smoking. Smoking by women wasn't so widely accepted then, and Dad was a little old-fashioned.

I did as Emily told me and liked it very much, but one day I was working on the utility porch and was smoking. I inhaled with a big draw. The next thing I remembered I was sitting with my back against the washing machine and I felt like hell.

Did you ever try to stand up when your feet felt like they were six yards below you? Then I got dizzy and felt I was going to be sick to my stomach. I knew where the sink was but I couldn't get my feet started that way. And there was a little room nearby. I knew I had better be going to it too.

That should have broken me of wanting to smoke, but thirty-three years later I am still smoking—but I always sit down.

Christmas Day I got sick and for two weeks all I wanted to eat was canned grapefruit. I had weighed one hundred and seventy-seven pounds for years but when I got up after two weeks in bed I only weighed one hundred and thirty-five pounds. When I started to get dressed I looked down and the folds of skin on my legs made them look like two accordians.

While I was sick I stayed with Mama in her apartment part of the house and she was the best little nurse.

When Mama moved in with us the welfare, or State Public Assistance as they call it today, paid her seventy dollars a month. After Dad passed away they cut it down to forty dollars. They said lots of widows take in relations and live off their welfare payments. It was a racket, they said.

I felt well enough, and we needed the money, so I went to work for Warren McDonald in his grocery store in Port Angeles. My sister Earline took Mama while I was on the job but I only got to work about six weeks because Mama kept running away. Earline lived on Peabody Street and with all the traffic it was too dangerous to leave Mama there where she might wander into the street every time she decided to leave.

Mama would simply wait until nobody was watching her and then she would go. The neighbors knew about her ways and would report where Mama was. She was always happy to see me and came home willingly. Maybe she liked the attention. Mama had always thrived on attention.

My family life and the Grange filled a lot of my time and I had the payments from Helen and Chad after they bought the store.

After it was dark Mama never tried to run away. She would read, play her piano then go to bed when she got sleepy. That made it nice for me because I was still secretary for Fairview Grange and I didn't have to worry about leaving Mama alone at nights when I went to the meetings. The Grange meant so much to me.

In September of 1948 I was elected, along with two other women, to put up a Fairview Grange booth at the Western Washington State Fair in Puyallup. Mama stayed with a good friend Mary Jarvis. I was gone a week. We old gals worked long hours and, believe it or not, took first prize. I still have my picture of our booth.

When school was out Emily's two boys would come up from Tacoma and stay with me. With them and with

Helen's three children right across the road I had a ball. The girls were wonderful to me to let me have the children. If you don't have them to do for when they are little, you don't have closeness when they are grown. All my grandchildren still mean so much to me.

In the fall of 1949 I received a letter from Bobbie in Alaska saying she was expecting a baby some time in December. She wanted me to come up and be with the two boys while she was in the hospital. I didn't know what to do. I was kept busier than cold water in a pan of hot grease, just taking care of Mama.

I went to the welfare people to see if I could put her in a nursing home until I got back from Alaska. Earline was working and had boarders too so she couldn't take care of Mama. When the welfare woman asked about Mama's other sons or daughters I said I had a brother living in Petersburg, Alaska, who was working in a logging camp. The old gal said, "Can't you just drop your mother off there to live with her son?" Well, I just pray I am never on welfare.

It seems that after my brother Alfred died and Mama could not support herself anymore a good friend of hers in Port Angeles got her on welfare. After Alfred's death Mama deeded her little home to Francis. Soon after that Mama asked welfare for a new roof and got it but the first strong wind blew a lot of it off.

One Sunday I took food, and Bill Gilliam and several neighbors got together and we had a dinner and they nailed the roofing down good and tight.

After Mama came to live with me, Francis sold Mama's house and went back to Alaska. The old welfare gal was sure mad. The welfare people thought Mama still owned the house and they were going to take it to pay for the aid they gave Mama. The woman threatened to get some men to pull our apartment Mama lived in away from my house, so they could take it to have in place of Mama's house on Pine Hill. I could tell you more about that old battle-ax but she isn't worth writing about.

I went to my friend-in-need Dr. James Hay. He said he would tend to getting Mama in the nursing home and if she wanted to come and live with me when I came back, and she was able to, he would see to that too.

I took Mama to the home. It was an old wooden building on Mount Angeles Road and had been the poor farm years ago. I stayed with her until it was time for her to go to bed.

I flew to Alaska in time for Christmas. Don's birthday was December 27 so I made a cake and a special dinner. Around seven o'clock Bobbie began having pains and she was walking from room to room to help the baby come. Don asked her why she didn't go up and down the stairs to the basement. Bobbie said, "Who's having this baby—you or me?"

Bobbie went to the hospital and about 10:30 that night the baby was born. It was their first little girl and Bobbie named her Pattie Rae. She said with two brothers Pattie Rae might act like a tomboy and her name would fit in better if she did.

In spite of his eagerness to have boys Don always babied Pattie, probably because she was born on his birthday and was their first little girl.

Chapter 23

I came back from Alaska sometime in January of 1950. I brought Mama home from the nursing home. Poor little thing, she was more confused than ever. She became quite ill and was in the hospital for a month. Dr. Hay said she would be much better off in the nursing home, so that's where she went when she left the hospital.

In April, I went into Port Angeles and took the exam needed to make me eligible to go from door to door to take the ten-year census. I passed and was assigned to the Blue Mountain, O'Brien, Township, and Deer Park Roads right in my own neighborhood. It was a lot of hard work and everybody had a dog or two to come bounding out to meet me.

I could fill a book with all the different people and their reactions to the census questions. Don't fool yourselves, girls. Men don't like to tell their ages any better than we do.

One old bachelor I had to call on was sure honest about how he felt. When I knocked on his door and told him I was the census taker he said, ''No woman comes in my house that I don't get what I want so either come in or set on the porch.''

Gosh! I sat on the lowest step of the porch! He answered all questions but his age. He said he was twenty-two and that was that! He was the oldest looking twenty-two-year-old I have ever seen.

A person had to watch those bachelors. Another old bachelor lived in a one-room house with nothing but a bed, two small tables, chairs, and a stove. In one corner was a chopping block set in a hole in the floor just cut to fit. He would bring a chunk of wood in as he needed it and chop it up for the stove.

I got out of the house all right but as I was walking to the car he said, ''You know, Emily, you sure got good looking legs,'' then before I could get the car door closed he pinched one of them.

I started going to dances and met some nice men. Roscoe Miles was one of them. His wife had passed away and he had three children—Harry, Jim and Mae. Mae was married and the two boys still lived with their dad.

The five main dance halls around Port Angeles were Fairview, Agnew, Pleasant Mountain, Dry Creek and Black Diamond. Fairview, I always thought, had the best floor. It was built in 1919. To build it Fairview Hall Association members signed notes for a specified amount of money then took the notes to the bank and the bank loaned money to the members for lumber and such. I expect other halls were built on the same plan.

The dance crowds were big in those days. In order to select the most desirable crowds and to avoid the fights public dance halls had, Pleasant Mountain formed its own dance club. I joined the club in 1948.

Here's something they did at dances years ago and, thank goodness, they don't do it today. The women always took paper and pencil along and, darn it, I can't remember what we called the paper or little book, or whichever we had, but it held our engagements for waltz or whatever dance some man had asked us to save for him.

Gosh, half the time the darn men forgot who they were suppose to dance with so they didn't show up and there you sat and waited, and had to say no to whoever else came over to ask you for a dance.

Benches were against both sides of the hall and the end opposite the entrance. The orchestra—usually at least a violin, piano, and drums—was along a part of one side. Women were suppose to sit and wait to be asked to dance. When midnight came it was time for supper upstairs. The meal was usually prepared by one person and the dancers paid about fifty cents for it.

One dance didn't do some of our family relationships much good. We had relatives visiting us for three weeks. The last Saturday they were with us there was a dance at Fairview Hall. The relations wanted me to go but all they had for transportation was a two-seated motorcycle. Dad told them, ''Take my car,'' and he said for me to go too. He would stay with our two girls born at that time.

I never thought about having to pay to get into the hall, and Dad didn't either. When we got to the hall the relations paid for their tickets and went inside. Boy, I didn't know what to do. I had no money and I hadn't learned to drive yet so I just stood there on the porch.

Pool at Olympic Hot Springs

After a while my cousin Nat came out and found me there, and was he ever mad at what happened! He paid for me to go in and also for the midnight lunch.

I never heard what Dad did but he was mad, and the company left the next day.

One of the homesteaders from the old days, Harve Anderson, his wife Anna, and his son Floyd had bought a farm in Indian Valley west of Port Angeles in 1909, and moved out there. I thought a lot of them and went out often to stay. Anna had always liked me and was good to me.

After Harve passed away I went out real often. Her son had married and Anna was all alone. She was in her eighties but still milked the cow and planted and took care of her garden. One way she got so much done was by careful scheduling.

One morning Anna told me to get breakfast for her while she milked the cow. I looked in the cupboard and there were seven different kinds of breakfast foods—one for each day of the week—so I picked out the one I liked best. That was on a Thursday and I had picked what was suppose to be her Monday's breakfast. It sure threw her schedule off.

Another day I was boiling potatoes in a kettle. Anna came in and said, "Land o'goshen! I never use that kettle!" She put the potatoes in another kettle to finish boiling.

Two other wonderful friends were Winfred and Margaret Doty. They lived in Port Angeles, I had known Winfred since 1901 when my family first came here. Margaret's folks were also homesteaders on Blue Mountain Road. I was lonesome and went to Dotys' a lot. I look back now and wonder how they stood me coming so often.

Not long after Dad passed away I needed to find work. There was no Social Security available to me and darn few people could qualify for welfare. I knew Jean Schoeffel as a girl, and she and her husband Harry needed help operating Olympic Hot Springs where I had spent a vacation with the Elwha Bunch.

During my stay at the hot springs in 1913 the pool was just a hole dug out of mud and banked with logs. We sat on the logs and slid down into the pool. If you had money you ate in the big tent with the tables and benches. If you didn't you fixed your own meals.

When I went to work there June 1, 1950, I couldn't believe the changes. There was a long building. It was the lodge. The downstairs was where you registered for your stay and use of the pool, or just lounged around and relaxed. The whole front was big windows that looked out on the beautiful concrete-lined pool. Upstairs were the dining room, kitchen and so forth. On each side of the pool were the dressing rooms with shower facilities. Under the dressing rooms on the west side, along Boulder Creek, was the "slab" where the help had rooms and bathtubs of hot water. Still farther down along the bank, under the slab, were the laundry tubs.

The road approached the hot springs along the west bank of Boulder Creek and you could look across the creek to the resort. Then the road crossed the creek on a bridge and started back along the opposite bank. The first five cabins you came to were real nice little houses—just like living down home, but they cost more to rent. Up on the hillside were about twenty single cabins.

It was hard work; more than twenty cabins to clean. I learned more about people and their ways in that four months than I had in all the fifty-three years of my life. One was always to knock on a cabin door to see if anybody was in there. Before I learned not to bounce in and out I found out a lot of things about the guests I shouldn't have.

I was paid one hundred dollars a month and my board. We worked real hard, seven days a week, and my weight went down to one hundred and thirty pounds. I always held the pillows with my chin when I put on the pillow slips, so I wore my double chin off too.

The biggest tip I received was five dollars. It was from a Japanese woman who came up to the hot springs every summer. She said it was the first time the bed was made so she could pull the covers up around her neck without her feet being left out.

You couldn't keep ash trays in the cabins so I replaced them with pretty clam shells. I was sure that was the answer to people taking the ash trays. But it wasn't; they took all the shells too.

Two women in succession were hired to do the laundry for the resort. They both were what I would call the "cat's pajamas." The good Lord sure wasn't thinking when he produced them. They were both very religious and I was taught to respect people and their different religions, but in this case I found it hard to do.

While I was at the hot springs my daughter Helen was in the hospital for an operation. Jean Schoeffel and I were talking about Helen and Jean said I could have Tuesday off to be with my daughter. The laundry woman found out about it and put a sign on a door, "Be good to Emily—her daughter is at death's door."

One day the laundry worker went to her cabin for her lunch and didn't come back to work so I went to see why. There she was, lying on the bed—drunk—praising the Lord and drinking the ammunition. She was a good worker but she had been "praising the Lord" too many times and had to be laid off.

The other laundry woman was tall and skinny. Jack, our handyman, saw her in the pool one early morning and told us that was the biggest water skipper he had seen up there. The water skippers were long-legged bugs with small bodies that skittered around on ponds and creeks.

She was over forty years old and had never been married. She was a fanatic about flowers, trees and other plants—pulling them apart to see if they were male or female. She told us everything living had sex.

Most of the help had their own room down on the "slab." The rooms got their name from being built on a big section of concrete below the men's dressing rooms.

The new laundry woman's room was down there and it was full of specimens. She would pull all sorts of things apart and try to see what sex they were—even rocks.

We had bathtubs on the slab. After work we could take hot mineral baths—if we could get enough water in the tub. Everytime we turned the water on old Julia would run out of her room and shut it off. Then she would tell Schoeffels she was tired because the help were taking baths at eleven o'clock at night, disturbing her sleep.

Harry came down to find out why we were bothering the woman so she couldn't sleep. We told him what she was doing. The next night Harry came down to see what was going on. Sure enough, as soon as we tried to get our tubs full of water, out came the woman. It was near time to close the hot springs for the season so Harry fired her and the rest of us took turns with the laundry.

We had bears. They came to eat out of the garbage barrels. A German woman staying at the resort made a cake and frosted it and put it out to cool. A bear found it and ate it. I don't know what she said in German, but she was sure mad.

I was still secretary of Fairview Grange so I went down twice a week after work to take care of that duty. One morning, real early, I was driving back and a deer crossed the road in front of me and right behind it was a cougar after the poor little thing.

I was going with Roscoe, who I had met at the dance, and he came up to the resort every Sunday and helped me with my work so we could have time to go for walks.

The Schoeffels were nice people to work for. I stayed there until the fifteenth of October when the summer season was over.

A few years later Olympic National Park closed down the resort and left the buildings to the weather. With no care they were badly damaged and then the remains were bulldozed into the pool and covered with dirt.

Chapter 24

Well, I reached 1952 and life didn't show any signs of slowing down although I was nearly sixty years old. In fact it turned out to be a very busy year.

In May I received a letter from Bobbie in Alaska saying she was expecting a baby once again, and again she wanted me to come up to be with the children while she was in the hospital. The baby was born May 28, a boy who was named Russell Don Conover.

After I came home a dear friend Anna Anderson asked me if I would go with her back to where she was born eighty-five years before in Rushville, Indiana. I was pleased she asked, and nothing would do but she would pay my way.

We went by train and stayed a month. I enjoyed my visit very much but it sure was different in the Indiana town. The house we visited was well built but there were rows of the houses so close together that the only yards were a small patch in front and one in back.

There was just one chain grocery store in Rushville, and were they ever proud of it! The kitchens had pitcher water pumps, the ones with long handles you lift then push down several times to bring water up from the well. Light in the kitchen came from a single globe in the middle of the ceiling. They were so surprised to think we had several aluminum kettles at home. They had only one, but the farm had acres of corn, and the best tasting tomatoes.

Roscoe and I were still going together and after I got home he said it was time we got married. I was fifty-eight years old and Roscoe was fifty-three. On November 27 we were married.

We had a big wedding at the Fairview Grange Hall. The hall was decorated with a background of fir trees, and fir trees formed an archway. The ceremony was under the arch. Upstairs, where we ate, the tables had white cloths on them and they looked beautiful. It was planned by my two dear friends Margaret Doty and Nell Sutter.

My daughter Emily and her husband Orel came up from Eugene, Oregon. After we had lunch and our wedding cake was cut, the Grangers came and we all

Roscoe and Emily's wedding photo: A new life

danced and it was great! Oh, yes, my mother, who was ninety-two years old, and Roscoe's mother, who was eighty-two, were both there.

When we started on our honeymoon, we stayed all night in a hotel in Port Angeles. That was only the second time I had stayed in a hotel since 1901 when our family first came here from Illinois.

We left for Victoria, Canada, across the Strait of Juan de Fuca from Port Angeles, the next morning and stayed all night in a hotel there. We planned to go to Nanaimo

A tree topping by Roscoe

the next morning but we missed the boat, so we got on a street car and rode out to the end of the line and back again.

The conductor was a Mr. Green. We got to talking with him and said we were on our honeymoon so Mr. Green said to us, "Mrs. Green and I went to Port Angeles and were treated so nice we would like you to come to our home tonight for dinner." I still think that was a wonderful thing for them to do. We went home the next day.

Roscoe's two boys were still at home with him. Harry was twenty-two years old and Jim was eighteen. His married daughter Mae was twenty. The boys lived with us for two years then Harry was married and Jim went to college in Portland, and later into the Army.

Roscoe was a logger. We got up at four in the morning when he was working in a logging camp run by Reid Priest, out by Forks, sixty miles southwest of Port Angeles. Then in 1959 he went to Skykomish in the northern part of the state to work for Glenn Priest, Reid's brother, who was running a logging camp there.

In 1960 Roscoe went to Wrangell, Alaska, in April to work in a logging camp. Bobbie and Don sent my sister Earline and myself airplane tickets so we could visit them. We went up in June.

Roscoe came to Anchorage July 1 and he, Earline and I went to Fairbanks four hundred miles away. It was smaller than Anchorage but interesting, especially its museum. We three later went from Anchorage to Homer, another four hundred miles.

Homer has a spit of land protecting its harbor, like we have in Port Angeles. While there we stayed with Lloyd Race, an old friend who used to live on Mount Pleasant Road east of Port Angeles. He took us to a crab cannery where king crabs were canned. They are delicious.

There was a general store down by the beach which was something else. Everything in there from soup to you-know-what—stacks of flour in sacks with a bolt of cloth on top, or nails and a big cheese and knife all in the same big box. By golly, it was worth the trip.

Earline had to go home. Roscoe was looking for work so we went to Juneau. Our friends Frank and Luella Rodgers were there. Frank was sawyer in a mill. The town had very little room for buildings. It was built on a mountain side and had seventy steps from one street to another.

No work for Roscoe in Juneau so Frank told him to try Sitka. They were logging there. We went down to the dock at Juneau to go to Sitka and it started raining. The stairs down to the dock had a roof over them, but just walking to the dock to get on the amphibious airplane it was raining so hard we were just soaked!

What an airplane ride that was! No dock at Sitka; just run the plane up on the beach, bumpity-bump, but I have liked the safe, solid feel of a beach ever since.

We got a two-by-four room in a hotel. Roscoe found work and left at 7 a.m. He went by power boat to an island where the company was logging. They were long days for me, with nothing to do. I paid one dollar and went into the famous Sitka Russian Church. I was lucky that day. They were showing robes. The robes were beautiful.

Sitka was the capital of Alaska until the big shots decided to move it to Juneau. The island was very pretty. It had a beautiful home for Senior Citizens. The Japanese owned a mill there.

A nurse owned a car so when she wasn't on duty, for a dollar apiece she took a carload of us around the island. I enjoyed seeing the totem poles carved by the Indians.

We only stayed a month in Sitka before Roscoe quit. Eating out and paying the hotel bill didn't leave us very much of Roscoe's paycheck.

We flew to Ketchikan and got a room in a hotel there. Roscoe went out looking for a job. We had been there three days when while Roscoe and I were eating lunch in a restaurant Mrs. Pat LaMae saw Roscoe and came over to our table. Roscoe had met Mr. and Mrs. LaMae when he was working at Wrangell in April. LaMae was head man in Alaska Logging Company.

Roscoe told Mrs. LaMae he was looking for work. She said not to worry, that she would go to the employment association and see what she could come up with. She was back in no time and said a foreman was needed at Campbell Camp out at Twelve-Mile Arm right away.

The Ellis Company had the franchise to fly to the Alaska Islands but had no plane at Ketchikan at the time. Mrs. LaMae said she knew a Swede named Ole who had a plane and would fly us to Twelve-Mile Arm. We found out later that the place was called that because the inlet was twelve miles long.

Anyway, we went to our room and packed our suitcases, paid our bill and walked down to the dock. I couldn't see any airplane but something was bobbing up and down on the water near the wharf. It turned out to be the plane. It held two passengers and it looked like an oversized mosquito to me.

Roscoe and I got into the thing, shut the door, put our seatbelts on, and Ole started the engine. He darn near drowned us just taking off. The spray washed over the plane.

The Ellis Company was required to fly all the way over water for safety. But not Ole. We were out over the water at first then he turned to go up over the mountains.

The door flew open and all Ole said was, "I should fix that door." We went so close to trees the wind from the plane made the limbs wiggle. Ole said, "If it's too cold for you I can shut the window." Gosh, for once in my life I couldn't say a darned word.

We at last got to Twelve-Mile Arm, but it was cloudy. Ole started down. He saw a blue spot and landed on the water and drifted over where four long logs had been tied together end-to-end. These were what you walked on over twenty-foot-deep water to the shore.

Lord, forgive my husband. I never have!

When we did get to shore two women were waiting for us. One woman said, "Are you Mrs. Miles?" I nodded and she said, "You are as white as a ghost. Come into the cookhouse for a cup of coffee."

Jim Campbell was manager of the camp. We were assigned to his brother-in-law's house. It was an old building that had been brought from Ketchikan on a scow. Like all of them at Twelve-Mile Arm it was a float house. A big cable tied from the house to a tree on shore kept it from going out with the tide.

We ordered supplies whenever the tugboat took a boom of logs to Ketchikan. We slept at the cabin but had to eat at the cookhouse until a boom of logs was ready to be taken in so we could get groceries delivered when it returned.

Mrs. Campbell was head cook. She was the manager's mother. Gosh, I couldn't eat a thing with twenty-five or thirty men looking at me, so Mrs. Campbell was nice enough to ask me to come and eat in the kitchen with the cook and help.

Juneau, Alaska

Chapter 25

The house we lived in on Twelve-Mile Arm had three rooms downstairs and an attic. The only way to the attic was a stairway out on the float, right in front of the kitchen window. The stairway had four steps up then a platform then more steps. There were a lot of seagulls around so I saved the kitchen scraps. After dinner I would put the scraps on the platform and in the morning, when the tide was out, I would throw the food out on the mud flat. I would call, "Come, babies, Come, babies!" and the gulls would fly down and have a feed.

One night, sometime after I had put the scraps on the platform, I went out in the kitchen and looked through the window and a black bear was on the platform eating the gulls' dinner. I hollered for Roscoe who came with a flashlight.

He went to the kitchen door and opened it and flashed the light on the bear. The bear jerked his head around and hit the window with a bang. Gosh! It scared me, but maybe not as much as it did the bear. He went down the stairs backwards and never came back again.

The electric light plant ran on diesel fuel and was way too small to serve all of us. The refrigerator would almost stop, then stand and rock a little, then take off again. Too many appliances on one circuit. When you plugged in your washing machine to wash and somebody else started their machine, your wringer and washer would stop. Sometimes it would be a half-hour before it would run again.

Every month a series of twenty-foot-high tides would come in for two or three days. The first morning it happened after we were there I opened the outside door to the house and the walk that connected us to the mainland was standing straight up and down. The walk was hinged where it was fastened onto the float but was loose where it lay about ten feet over on the bank alongside the house.

The sight scared me out of my wits. I just prayed that when the tide went out the cable holding the house to the shore wouldn't break.

Most of the people who lived around us were nice but a dad of two kids was a real gooney. The kids, a sixteen-

Floating home at 12-Mile Arm, Alaska

year-old boy and a ten-year-old girl, had to eat at 4:30 every night, before their dad got home, then either go to a shack that had no windows in it where they slept or play outdoors. Their dad wouldn't eat if the kids were at the table.

People at the cookhouse warned us not to leave our door unlocked if we went for a walk, indicating the kids might steal something. I had ordered four dollars worth of stamps and left them in the house when I walked over to the commissary for my mail. I had not locked the door. My stamps were gone when I got back.

I felt sorry for these kids, the way they had to get out of their house in the evenings, and, since Roscoe was tired from his hard work and went to bed as soon as he was through eating, I decided to ask the kids down to the house to play three-handed pinochle with me. Do you know, I never lost a thing after that, and they came down anytime they wanted to.

Our cookstove burned oil. I guess everybody's did. Anyway, when the tugboat was coming back from Ketchikan with the barge, it had our barrels of stove oil on it and hit a bad storm. All the barrels of oil were washed overboard. Jim Campbell had lots of diesel oil so that's what we had to burn in our oil stoves. It was awful. It smoked and had no heat to it.

It rained some every day at Twelve-Mile Arm. We would hang our washing out on a line to dry then run and bring it in when the rain started, then run back out and hang it out again when the rain quit. Most of the time we could get the laundry dry.

Mrs. Campbell, who was the cook, made pies really often. I guess the crust wouldn't even make good cookies. Roscoe said when the help ate their lunch at noon they ate what was inside the pie and threw away the crust.

One night when Mrs. Campbell made her pies, ready for the next day, she put them on a table to cool and went to her bunkhouse to sleep. Some of the men happened to look in the cookhouse window and saw the pies. They broke the window and ate the filling out of all the pies and left the crusts. Mrs. Campbell was madder than a wet hen, probably mostly because of the insult to her baking.

People took turns having dances at different homes on Saturday nights but we were never invited. Later I was told why. It seems like whenever an airplane landed on the water and let the passengers off the women all watched through binoculars. If the party arriving didn't have a case of beer along it was considered they didn't drink, so they were not invited to the dances.

A neighbor next to me—her house was on real ground—had a dance one night at her home. She was a native but her husband was a white man. Anyway, she called me over to her house the next day and, by golly, a big heater stove was knocked over on its side and the liquor bottles left were higher than two Irishmen could shake hands over.

We were at Twelve-Mile Arm five weeks when one day the assistant manager of the logging operation came over to our place and told me Roscoe had been hurt. They had called for one of the Ellis planes to pick him up and take him to the hospital in Ketchikan. I was to get a suitcase packed and be ready when the plane got there.

Roscoe had fallen and twisted his knee real bad. Three of the women came over and helped me pack enough clothes for the trip. In the rush they didn't make sure things, like stockings, matched so I was dressed a little odd in Ketchikan.

The first night in Ketchikan I stayed in a hotel near the hospital. I was in Roscoe's room when the doctor came in. Roscoe and I talked to him and he told us Roscoe would be in the hospital longer than I could afford to stay in the hotel.

Down by the Ketchikan River was a place called Ketchikan Rooming House. I got my suitcase and went down there. Gosh, one little room, one light in the middle of the ceiling, a two-burner stove—only one worked and the stove sat on the only table in the room—an old iron cot for a bed, one sink—the kind you usually wash your hands in, not dishes—and two apple boxes nailed to the wall for dish cupboards. It was like homestead days again.

Anyway, I cooked my dinner and ate it and put my dishes in the hand-sink and was having a cigarette when somebody upstairs pulled the plug in their sink after washing their dishes. All the water flushed down into my

Ketchikan, Alaska, 1960

sink. It was the first and only time I ever had a dishwasher.

I had no heat, only my one burner on the stove. My bed was against the wall next to the hall. The community biffy was down the hall, past my room. I don't know what those older people drank or ate but they shuffled down and back all night long. But I never did see even one of them. They stayed in their rooms in the daytime.

The Ketchikan River was real close to the rooming house and the falls were beautiful. It was so interesting to watch the fish. They were on their way to spawn and tried so hard to get up over the falls. Many died trying. We think sometimes God is pretty hard on us but He is also hard on the fish.

The main street to the docks was narrow. It was tunneled through a cliff. A lot of the houses were built on rock above the tunnel.

When we were at Twelve-Mile Arm, Helen shipped a trunk of clothes and things for me to sew on. I made some roses out of fiber cloth, sprayed a pretty bottle gold color and sold them for five dollars. It was the only time I ever received money for my handiwork.

I went back to Twelve-Mile Arm to pack the rest of our things before Ross got out of the hospital. Then I returned to Ketchikan.

Alaska totem in early 1900s photo

84

Chapter 26

Roscoe recovered and was out of the hospital. It was December 1960 and no work until spring dried and thawed the area out. One night in the Ketchikan Rooming House was enough for Roscoe. We packed, put the trunk on the boat, and flew home.

Even if we could collect higher unemployment in Alaska by staying there until spring, I was glad to go home. I worried about my mother. She was one hundred years old and not too well.

Helen, Chad, and their children were glad to see us. The house didn't go up and down with the tide, and nobody was shuffling up and down the hall at night. Of course, I had lost my dishwasher.

I always wanted a house with a big front room. In February we hired two carpenters Ed Bruchner of Sequim and Paul Cameron of Fairview. They added twelve feet to the width of the front room which made it twenty feet by twenty-five feet with three big windows. I still just love it.

By March Roscoe needed work so we drove to Forks to see the Brager brothers Lawrence and Clarence who

Forks in the 1940s

owned a logging operation. Roscoe had worked in the woods with them twelve years when the Bragers first moved to Forks. When Roscoe asked Clarence for work Clarence told him he didn't have to ask about working for them, just be there Monday morning. That was wonderful.

We had to look for a place to live. It was too far to run back and forth to R Corners. So in March of 1961 we moved to Forks. My grandson Dale from Alaska lived in our house and went to Peninsula College in Port Angeles while we were gone.

We found a house to rent in Forks but it wasn't much. The heater and kitchen stoves burned gas, which was new to me. They were both old stoves. The heater blew gas all over the front room. The kitchen was so small that if you opened the kitchen stove's oven door it was about an inch from the refrigerator door.

I was lonesome and the neighbor next to us never spoke so I didn't either, until one day I was making bread.

There was no heat gauge on the oven so you opened the door and, like on a wood stove, put your hand into the oven to tell if it was hot enough for baking. I did this and the oven wasn't hot enough so I shut the door. I took about two steps and the darn stove exploded and blew the oven door against the refrigerator. All the stove lids flew off and the explosion broke two windows and scared me out of my wits.

I ran out onto the back porch and Edna Haag the next-door neighbor hear the awful noise and came running over to see what happened. She said, "Bring your bread over to my house and bake it." There's always something good comes out of something bad. We got acquainted and are still good friends.

The landlady never did get around to fixing the oven. An old gasoline-motor-operated washing machine that was sure hard to get started added to the problems. The piece that held the wringer in place was broken so if you let go of it the wringer kept on going and water went all over the floor.

When the bed broke down one night and Roscoe had to get an apple box to hold it up—that was it! Roscoe thought I had better find another place to rent.

We were only out at Forks about a month when Clarence Brager passed away. Poor Clarence had suffered for years from an accident to his head that occurred while he was working at their logging camp. The Good Lord was with us. Before we found a place to rent, Ella, Clarence's widow, came over to see if we would move into her house. She was lonesome.

The house had an apartment which contained one big room with a davenport bed in it, a nice bathroom, a kitchen with an electric stove, and baseboard electric heat throughout the house. That was where we lived.

Ella had three children—a girl married, one in high school, and a six-year-old boy Bill. It was awful hard for Bill to understand why his dad had passed away. When he came home from school I always tried to have cookies or something' for him. When Roscoe came home after work Bill would come over and bring his games and we would play with him. Bill is a grown man now, and a fine one too, and I am so glad he still calls me Grandma.

I don't know how to express myself about the four years we lived in Forks. I loved every day of it. They are real people. It was then a logging town with a main business street about three blocks long. Some business ran over onto another street. Few men ever dressed up. In fact most of them were loggers and after work just stayed in the striped hickory shirts and denim pants cut off short so they wouldn't get tangled in the brush while the men worked in the woods. After work their spiked boots, called caulks or corks, were usually changed for comfortable shoes but that was about all.

Logging is hard work and about all a logger feels like when he is finally through for the day is a little relaxation and some sleep. But they still found time to be friendly and helpful to their neighbors and community.

I joined the Garden Club. It was very active. I learned how to arrange bouquets, sew, make table favors, plant and make things grow. We took many interesting trips to the ocean and other beaches.

Once a year the club had a carnival. The displays were great. The paintings some of those women did were beautiful. You see, lots of the women had lived in Forks before there was a road around Lake Crescent and without an easy way to get out of the area they were, you might say, "housed in." They really created for their own entertainment and did just great.

I also joined, and became secretary to, the Hospital Guild. They have breakfasts at no charge but many of the Forks people came and gave more than the price of a ticket, and all the proceeds went to the Forks Community Hospital. We made lots of lap quilts and visited the patients. It makes me feel good all over again just to write about it.

On December 7, 1961, my daughter Helen phoned and said my mother was quite sick at the nursing home. It was Friday afternoon so when Roscoe came home from work I had dinner ready and we ate and left for Port Angeles. Little Mother passed away that day. She was one hundred and one years, three months, and four days old.

Mama was only five feet, two inches tall, and weighed one hundred and two pounds. She was very well educated, gave piano lessons, and was a little brick when it came to facing up to things. She was a wonderful mother.

Mama's father Count Julius Von Henchell of Hamburg, Germany, died of tuberculosis when Mama was only one year old. Why, I don't know, but she was so sure she would someday get a fifteen thousand dollars inheritance from Germany. It never happened.

Long before we left Forks in December 1965 the people there had made the rugged little town a home for us. There were Paula and Logan Kaas. We are still very good friends. We also met Dr. and Mrs. Edward F. Leibold. I must not forget Lawrence Brager, who took over and managed the camp very well after Clarence passed away; Ella Brager, now Mrs. Warren Paul too. I feel like she is just another one of my girls. Jessie Brager, Lawrence's wife, is another one of my girls out in Forks.

Lawrence and others gave us a farewell party before we left. If I were a young person and had to move I would move to Forks, Washington.

Chapter 27

The 1960s didn't start too well for me. Mama died, in 1963 I had an ulcer operation and one third of my stomach removed, in 1964 a doctor stripped my left leg of varicose veins, in 1967 he operated on my right leg and I sure had bum luck with that operation.

The doctor had told the nurse to get me up the first night. Gosh—those poor nurses—my leg opened up and bled all over them and the bed. The next morning the doctor stuck his head in the door and told the nurse to get me up again. The head nurse came in to help and that time when I put my foot on the floor the blood filled my new bedroom slipper and went all over those nurses again.

They put me back in bed and called the doctor. He was there in fifteen minutes. The nurse put a tourniquet on my leg above the knee. When the doctor came in he said to the nurse, "For a vein, a tourniquet goes below, not above, the incision. Didn't you learn that in training?"

Believe it or not, the nurse said to the doctor, "Yes, but if you had read Mrs. Miles' chart you would have known she is a bleeder!"

The long and the short of it is I was laid up for twelve weeks.

But there was a big bright spot at the end of it all. In June 1967 Roscoe bought a new Chevrolet pickup truck and a little trailer house. It had a bed, sink, stove, a table, and that was all. He wanted to drive up the Alcan Highway to Anchorage. The doctor said not to go, that it would be too hard on me. But you know men—when they make up their mind it's made up.

We left home June 17, 1968, and stopped at Sequim and had lunch with Mr. and Mrs. Frank Lysall. We took the ferry at two in the afternoon from Port Townsend across Admiralty Inlet to Whidbey Island. If you knew Roscoe as well as I do, you would know he would be first one on the ferry. That didn't turn out to be so good. The water was so rough waves splashed onto our truck.

We drove to Hope, British Columbia, the first day and stopped at a very nice campsite there. June 18 at 9:30 in the morning we left camp and followed up through the Fraser Valley. That alone was worth the trip. We had lunch at 100-Mile House. We drove until eight in the evening and stayed at Ten-Mile Camp, measured from Quinell. It was raining, cold, and the mosquitoes were thick.

The morning of the nineteenth we drove to Bear Lake. There were fifty-nine camping units and twenty-four tables. Then on over the Rocky Mountain Pass. It was just beautiful. We stayed all night at Pine Hill. Acres of wheat were just coming up there. We had traveled nine hundred and fourteen miles so far. It was Thursday the twentieth and we were two hundred and forty-five miles from Dawson Creek.

The winters are long so when summer comes the road crew works hard and long hours. There was a piece of only one-way road and we were almost through when a car from California came right for us. Roscoe darn near tipped us over trying to dodge the car.

The swerving broke a screw holding the top of the stove and it came off. All the curtains came down and it broke some dishes. We stopped at the next service station. It was called Ev and Buck's Bunny Cafe. I was in for coffee and was telling them about the wrong-way driver. Ev said, "All people from California and New York are—you know what." Even after the near-accident I didn't think they were that bad.

Gosh, we stopped at an Esso station for gas and with no toilet in the trailer I was, of course, looking for a toilet. I got Roscoe to ask where it was because I couldn't see any. The manager told him, "It is over there behind that building."

I went over there and you will never believe me, he had made an outdoor pit toilet out of two fifty-five-gallon oil drums. One he buried sitting upright with both ends cut out. The other he only cut the bottom out and one side. It was on top of the buried one, with the upper end used as a roof.

The seat was a blown-up inner tube out of a car tire and it was all that kept you from ending up in the bottom barrel. This is the God's truth.

I looked at that seat and thought about the fifty-five-gallon drum hole. I knew where I would be if the air came out of the inner tube. I decided not to take the chance. There was a two-plank walkway up to the outhouse and the planks were pretty far apart, so I just used the crack in between.

We stopped one night at Lairds River. It's a big river and was one of the crew camps when they built the Alcan Highway. About a quarter of a mile from the river were some hot springs. It's all marshy tundra ground so they built a two-board walk out to the springs.

There was a little house to change clothes in. It had two long benches back to back—one for men and one for women—and no partition between them, just a high back on the benches. Men sat on one side to change and women on the other.

I thought I would never get to go in the pool. Every time I got started undressing some man would come in the door and pass by the women's bench to the men's side. Pretty soon an older woman came in and was watching me. She just shed her clothes before God and everybody.

Then she came over to me and said, "God made us all, Honey, so just go ahead and undress." She was nice and she stood in between me and that outside door while I changed.

When I got out to the pool I found out you could sit on the ground and put your feet in. The water was pretty darn warm too. I didn't know how deep it was and I don't swim, so a man on the other side of the pool swam over to me and said, "Come on, Grandma, I'll help you in and out again." Two nice people.

The hot springs must have been a treat for our Army boys building the highway.

White Horse was a nice little town but being Sunday only one grocery store was open. On our way to White Horse was a beautiful place called Miles Canyon. Roscoe was sure some of his relations had discovered it. It's a wonderful drive around the big lakes near White Horse and real nice people at the Customs Station.

We stopped to eat lunch and dinner at one place and they had potato salad on the menu. Well, I learned an easy way to make potato salad—one scoop of mashed potatoes, a gob of mayonaise and one sprig of parsley.

We drove for miles never saying a word. How God ever gave my husband such wonderful eyes I'll never know. If I said I saw something, Roscoe had already seen it. But

Board walk to Hot Springs

one day, about ten feet below the road, in the tundra was one of the biggest moose I have ever seen. When I told Roscoe he stopped so quick I darn near hit the windshield. He jumped out and got a picture of it.

We stopped at Tok Junction and called my daughter Bobbie in Anchorage. We had a hot bath and a nice dinner in a motel near Tok before going on to Anchorage the next day.

The road from White Horse to the Alaska border was what I would say, "like a washboard." The bouncing wore out the elastic straps that held my brassiere up and everything was as far down as they could go.

Don, Bobbie's husband, took a day off from work and the next morning after my call they started out early to meet us. They, of course, didn't know what our truck looked like, only that it had a Clallam County license plate. They saw one and turned around and caught up but it wasn't us.

Then as we were driving along a car went past us. The window was down and Bobbie's head stuck out. She was yelling, "Mama, Mama!" We followed them and pretty soon they turned off the road for lunch. Bobbie had fixed a tasty picnic. Linda my grandson's wife was with them. In spite of all the wonderful things we saw on the trip seeing them was the best!

Chapter 28

Well, at last we were in Bobbie and Don's home! My grandchildren were glad to see us. And Bobbie's house is only twelve blocks from downtown so I hiked down to the Penney's store and bought two new brassieres.

Roscoe and I decided to go out to Bobbie and Don's homestead and fish in the lake. Don said for us to take a gun because they were having trouble with a porcupine that was trying to chew its way into the house.

Well, we forgot the gun and we just got in bed one night when we heard the darn thing chewing the lumber right where the gas line for the cooking range came into the house. Roscoe pulled on his longjohns and went out after the porcupine with a club and a flashlight. I learned one thing—my husband could really swear! What with his swearing and pounding he killed the porcupine and we got to sleep.

We drove to Homer with our trailer and camped out at our old friend Lloyd Race's ranch. It's pretty there along the saltwater. We dug clams, went fishing for salmon and had lots of those wonderful king crabs. Lloyd had a furnace in his basement and never had to buy coal for it. He just took his truck and gathered it off the beach where it sloughed off from the bluffs along the water.

Our next stop was Seward. This was after the awful earthquake on Good Friday in 1964. Seward was as changed as Anchorage was. In Seward where the dock and railroad had been, everything was gone—train and all, in 90 feet of water.

Some friends who lived near Bobbie in Anchorage had given us the key to their cabin at Kenai Lake. So after a stop there we went back to Bobbie's with a big mess of fish.

When we were ready to leave Anchorage for home Bobbie and Don had a farewell party for us in their back yard. We had lots to eat and a good time. It was still light out at 10:30 p.m.

We started home. I wanted us to drive to Hains, Alaska, where we could take a ferry down the Narrows to Kelsey Bay on Vancouver Island in British Columbia, then drive to Victoria and ferry across the Strait of Juan de Fuca home. The ferry trip down the Narrows would

Totem of Alaska Indians

save us a thousand miles of driving, but Roscoe wasn't so sure he wanted to.

When we got near Hains Junction, Yukon Territory, Roscoe, on his own, decided to go to Hains, Alaska, and take a chance on getting on a ferry. He said I had worn him down.

Hains, Alaska, is a small town on a hillside. It had one

business street, one theater, etc. The only place to camp, if you had a trailer, was at Chilkoot Lake about eight miles out of town. We waited there a week before there was a ferry with room for us.

All week, as each trailer came into camp, Roscoe went right over to see where the people came from and where they were going. I think all lawyers should come from Oklahoma like Roscoe did. They know all about you before you know what's going on.

The trip on the Narrows was just beautiful, lots of green islands and blue water. There was a piano on the ferry and I was so lonesome for my piano. Gosh, I sure wanted to play that piano, but I was afraid to.

We could sleep in our trailer, but not cook so we ate upstairs, had good food too. There were so many trailers down below, and so close together, that when you left your trailer and got upstairs you had most of the cars and trailers all polished with your front or behind.

We went to Prince Rupert on the British Columbia mainland and got on the Canadian ferry Queen of Prince Rupert and rode twenty hours to Kelsey Bay on Vancouver Island. The ferry was clean and had good food too. We drove about two hundred miles down the island to Victoria and waited again to see if we could get on a ferry, to cross the Strait for home. We did and got to Port Angeles at 9:30 p.m.

It was the most wonderful trip any two people could ever wish to have. Everybody was glad to see us home. Our longtime neighbors and friends, Sutters, had a party for us at their home August 24.

Well we reached the mark—sixteen years since we both said, "I do," and they had been eventful and happy years. Then came the word *retirement*.

Women never really retire. The only difference to the wife when the husband retires is that she gets a lunch for him at noon instead of putting up his lunch the night before and her getting use to having him bouncing in and out all day long. That's the reason women last longer—they don't have to go through the retirement change.

Eskimo Russian Orthodox Church, Kuskokwim River, Alaska

Chapter 29

Well, my married life so far with Ross has been like a kite in a March wind—tossed about. There have been experiences I never had before, and it has been wonderful.

In 1965—fourteen years ago—we had to learn how to retire. We have been lucky. We have lots of company dropping in, which is a big help. Ross has a huge lawn to mow and gardens to take care of. He cuts hay for people and does plowing for others.

We can two hundred quarts of vegetables and fruit every year. Ed Hamilton, a friend, goes elk hunting every fall and brings me the neck from the elk. This makes ten quarts of mincemeat.

We go clam digging on the ocean beach at Kalaloch with our dear friends Paula and Logan Kaas of Forks. One time we were digging clams and I spotted a person digging right in front of us. I said to Ross, "Look at that girl's pretty curly hair hanging almost to her waist." While we were still admiring the hair the clam digger turned around and it had a mustache. That was a bit of a shock seeing such long hair on a boy for the first time.

Soon after retirement we formed a little orchestra. Fritz Sutter played the violin, Jerry Staudenraus was our drummer, and I played the piano. Bill Davidson played the guitar but after his marriage we had to find another guitar player. We were lucky enough to locate Don Ford, also his sister Alice Neas who plays the bass guitar. We played twice at Clallam Bay, once at the Neah Bay Air Force Station, once at the Sequim-Dungeness Irrigation Festival, and at many home gatherings and Grange affairs.

We still play at nursing homes. My daughter Helen will say to me, "Are you playing for the old folks today? You know, you are older than most of them in the nursing homes"—and then she laughs.

In December of 1972 I went to Swedish Hospital in Seattle and had an operation on my hip. I was there for nineteen days. The doctors and nurses were wonderful to me. One day I was walking down the hall with my walker—a frame of metal tubing to lean on to steady yourself—when a nurse asked me to go into a room with her. A man was in the bed and the nurse said to him, "This woman is eighty years old and walks twice a day. You are in your sixties and won't get up and even try to walk for us.'"

The man grunted and turned over. The next day there was a rap on my open door. The man was there with his walker. He walked every day after that.

That hip operation was one of the best things that ever happened to me. Ross said one day to me, "You know, I think that operation helped your disposition too."

Bobbie and Don came down from Anchorage in 1976 and while they were with us we called in our friends and we all helped them celebrate their thirty-fifth anniversary.

Ross was in the Coast Guard in 1920 and went to Nome on a ship called the *Bear*. He always wanted to go back again. There are excursions from Anchorage to Nome so during the summer of 1978 Ross and I flew to Anchorage

Emily and Roscoe: 25th Anniversary

and Bobbie and Don went with us to Nome.

We panned gold, went inside an igloo, saw some Eskimo dancers and saw their beautiful carved ivory. The buildings are on steel pilings on account of the permafrost. Wood pilings sink in no time.

We then flew to Kotzebue. The mounted wild animals in the museum there looked so natural you just expected them to start moving. We enjoyed the evening entertainment there too. They had a blanket toss game, using the blanket to throw people into the air and then catching them in the same blanket. Don even helped hold the blanket.

The Eskimos danced. They came into the room and sat on the floor. One little old-looking Eskimo woman was with them. Her husband had to help her up but when the music started for the dance she slowly waddled over to where they were dancing. And when the band hit a certain beat that little one came to life—and was she ever good! After the dancers were through they sat down on the floor again and I had to go over and tell her how good she did. She took hold of my hand and said, ''You are a sweet girl.''

When my brother Francis who lived in Anchorage had his eightieth birthday my sister Earline and I flew up to spend it with him. He was so pleased it was worth the trip although I hate to fly. Francis is ninety years old now and he and his wife Ruth live with Ruth's daughter Doris in Blyth, California.

To sum it all up, I still have three wonderful daughters, Emily, Helen and Bobbie; nine grandchildren; and I get to see them often although Bobbie still lives in Alaska and Emily lives in Oregon. Helen is close; she is a neighbor.

The band dressed to play at Sequim Festival. From left, Bill Davidson, Emily, Fritz Sutter, Nell Sutter, Jerry Staudenraus.

Chapter 30

I am now eighty-six years old. I find it hard to know how to finish my story.

It has been a good down-to-earth life for me. I've had my ups and downs but if we really stop to think about it, there's nothing so bad but what some good comes out of it. There are twenty-five in my family to love, including my dear sister Earline and brother Francis.

I couldn't have had a better place to live than good old Port Angeles. It sure looks different than it did on September 21, 1901, when we arrived from Illinois.

If we listen to the television and believe all we read in the newspapers I'll swear we wouldn't believe there are any good people left but there are lots of them yet. There are lots more good people than there are bad ones. Amen.

In our home at R Corners, Ross and I have lots of company and many friends, both young and old, and we sure love it. The world is changing and I think it will be harder for the young people of today than it was for us older ones. We had security and *LOVE*.

Hard work, yes, and very little education or money, but we were appreciative of the nice things that *did* come to us.

My daughter Helen planned a surprise party for me on my eighty-fifth birthday last year. She called my other girls, Bobbie in Anchorage and Emily in Oregon, and they came as part of the surprise. Emily's two sons came with her. All in all, counting our good friends here, and counting Ross and me, there were fifty people at the party. They rolled the carpet up, put it behind the davenport, pushed the dining room table against the wall, and we were ready for dancing.

Our little orchestra that night consisted of Fritz Sutter and Steve Hermann on violins, Don Ford on guitar, Alice Neas on bass guitar, and myself on piano. Ted Hermann, Steve's dad, helped at times on his mouth harp and our friend Glenn Williamson helped on his clarinet.

We played for three and a half hours. There were so many they took turns dancing and visiting so everybody could get their share of turns around the floor. I haven't seen such quantities of food at a party since the Fourth of July picnics in the good old days. It was beautiful and one of my happiest birthdays. I hope everybody knows how much I appreciate it.

There are times, I think, when it would be better if we didn't have birthdays. Lots of people worry about their age. At eighty-six I have done many things in recent years I dreamed about doing when I was young.

So live each day and don't be afraid to grow old.

THE END